If You Preach It, They Will Come

Preaching the Word
for Year C as Listeners Like It

Eduardo A. Samaniego, S.J.

STONEWALL PRESS
PAVING YOUR WAY TO SUCCESS

Printed in the United States of America

Library of Congress Control Number: 2018935385
eBook: 978-1-948172-18-9
Softcover: 978-1-948172-19-6
Hardcover: 978-1-948172-20-2

 **STONEWALL PRESS**
PAVING YOUR WAY TO SUCCESS

Stonewall Press
363 Paladium Court
Owings Mills, MD 21117
www.stonewallpress.com
1-888-334-0980

TABLE OF CONTENTS

ACKNOWLEDGMENTS

I want to thank a number of people who have influenced me and taught me to be the preacher that I am becoming. I thank my parents, whose faith in "Our Lord" planted the seed of my faith in Jesus. My father also gave me a book when I was a teenager many years ago: <u>Public Speaking as Listeners Like It!</u>,[1] a book formerly used by Toastmasters, a club that helps train public speakers. I never joined the club, but I always use the four rules in this simple book whenever asked to present myself in public.

I also thank Rev. Joe Powers, S.J., who, in a Christology class, gave us three questions to use as a test of an effective Evangelizing presentation. He embodied what he taught. May he rest in Peace.

Next, I want to thank Margie Brown, adjunct professor at the Pacific School of Religion in Berkeley, California. She overcame severe physical problems due to Muscular Dystrophy and became a tremendous Storyteller, Teacher and Evangelist in her ministry as a clown. She taught me to ask: "From what voice am I speaking?"

I want to thank Sr. Barbara Goergen, O.S.F., a Franciscan Sister of Rochester Minnesota, who listens to my homilies before I give them. She thinks and reasons in ways different from mine. From her faith and feedback I have learned to refine my homilies and to connect better with the people who "hear" differently than I do.

I thank Christ the King for encouraging me to be creative. Finally, I wish to thank Frs. Tom Smolich, S.J., Mick McCarthy, S.J., and Tom Reilley, S. J. for freeing me so that I could write this book.

---

1   Richard C. Borden, <u>Public Speaking as Listeners Like It!</u>, (New York and London, Harper & Brothers, 1935)

INTRODUCTION

When I studied Theology, there was a word that drew me and it has never left me: Presence. Theology and ministry are about Presence. Preaching, too, is very much about Presence.

Presence is what creates a people. Presence is the reality to which man[2] must attune himself if he is to live at all, for there is no solitary life... Presence is the begetter of theology..., which is not a science of the divine subject... Theology is not to know God but to be aware of being grasped and called to do the will of God in History...[3]

I have been a Jesuit for thirty-seven years and will celebrate twenty-eight years of ordained ministry. After twelve years as vicar and pastor of Christ the King Catholic Church in San Diego, and in my first year at Most Holy Trinity Church in San Jose, I feel "grasped and called" to share a way of organizing and structuring a homily that is both practical and learnable and is adaptable to the preacher's own personality and style.

Not wanting to reinvent the wheel in this book, I desire to give the prospective preacher a simple method of checking oneself in one's organization to guarantee an interesting, provocative, and faith-evoking method of preparing a homily or sermon. I also want to show how the use of "stories" enhances one's ability to help the congregation build a bridge from the Scriptures, or "THE STORY," to their own stories.

To illustrate the power of story, let me share with you a story that is a source of wonderful imagination and inspiration to me.

---

2   Whenever I quote directly from a person or source, I will write in the language they used. In my own writing, however, I shall use inclusive language.

3   Samuel Terrien, The Elusive Presence, (San Francisco: Harper and Row, 1978) pp. 124, 140, and 143.

A boy was playing in an old building and wandered into a room that happened to be the studio of a sculptor. He stayed and watched as the hammer and chisel skillfully chipped away at the great piece of marble. The boy left and did not return to the studio for weeks.

When he did return, he stood in the doorway gaping at the lion which stood before him. Walking in with eyes gleaming he asks the sculptor, "How did you know there was a lion in the marble?" The sculptor responded with a smile, "Before I knew there was a lion in the marble, I had to sit before the great block for hours. I would get up and look at it as the sun began to rise. I would sit during the noon-time rays. I would sit before it as the sun began to set. I then discovered that I had a lion in my heart, and this lion recognized the lion in the marble begging me to set it free. Then, all I had to do was remove what wasn't lion.[4]

The preacher must sit with both the block of marble that is one's life and the block of marble that is Scripture. Christ is already there in one's heart of hearts. Once the preacher discovers the Christ in his or her heart, then Christ can be recognized in the text of the Scriptures and in the text of one's life begging the preacher to be set free. The rest is easy: chip away what isn't of Christ.

I will not go into the details of how I prepare spiritually, i.e. contemplate the marble of my life and of the Scriptures to deliver the homily or sermon. I presume we preachers are people of prayer that encounter the living God, through whom we breathe and have our being. I also presume that we read, reread, study, and struggle with the Scriptures while praying them all week. Finally, I presume that we know and love God's people and that we are as humble walking with them as we are walking with God.

Having said this, I will not presume that we are as structurally prepared as we are spiritually prepared to deliver what God wants us to say. My hope is to help us preachers build on our own experience and open ourselves to effective structures and methodologies for getting the Word across to people eager to get it.

---

4   Henri Nouwen, <u>Clowning in Rome</u>, (Garden City, New York: Image Books, 1979) pp. 87 and 103.   Paragraph two has been adapted.

The first part of the book is a manual in which you will find four points to an interesting talk, three questions for an effective Evangelizing event, some thoughts on the use of story, and some helpful points from the Myers-Briggs Psychological Typing[5] that can enhance one's communication with the vast variety of people in our congregations, who process words and ideas differently from us as preachers. It concludes with helpful suggestions for discovering a theme for the homily, based upon the Scriptures used, and for keeping files on what and for whom you have preached.

The rest of the book will present examples of homilies that people said had impacted them. They are from the three-year cycle of Lectionary Readings. The concluding bibliography should provide a wealth of sources from which the avid preacher can better prepare to fulfill one's ministry of Word. In so doing let us remember:

"Preach the Word always, and if necessary, use words."[6]

May God's glory and honor be served.

---

5   Dr. Isabel Myers and Dr. Briggs along with Dr. David Keirsey and Dr. Marilyn Bates have studied the ways different individuals take in reality, process it, and respond to it. Their work is based in Carl Jung's theories of Psychological Types.
6   St. Francis of Assisi

CHAPTER ONE

THE FOUR RULES

"When you seek me with the whole of your heart, I will be found of you, says Yahweh." (Jer 29: 13-14)

In the foreword of <u>Public Speaking as Listeners Like It</u>!, you will find: "If you apply these principles, your listeners will like you. They will believe you. They will understand you. They will follow you. And these listener responses *you must get*. Unless you get them, your speech is not a speech. It is a mere performance."[7]

How many "mere performances" have been witnessed over the centuries of preaching in the Church? How many outstanding homilies or sermons[8] have been proclaimed throughout those same centuries? How many unconvincing words have been uttered without impact, without passion, and even without faith in the words spoken? How many faith-filled and faith-inspiring, passionate homilies have been delivered?

It is true that we are not talking about a speech when we say "homily." But a homily or sermon is still public speaking, so why not use the principles of good public speaking as one prepares to let God speak through the preacher? Why not adapt the principles that dynamic worldly speakers and holy preachers have used for years?

The four principles of good public speaking are the following: 1.) Ho Hum! 2.) Why did you bring this up? 3.) For instance... 4.) So What! Let us look at each principle more closely.

---

7   Borden, pg. i
8   I will use "homily" where both homily or sermon can be interchanged, because in my Catholic tradition, people are more used to hearing this term.

First, "Ho hum" is about getting the interest of the listener right away. There are many ways to get this, some of the most common ways are quotes, songs, jokes, newspaper headlines, magazine, television, flash cards and stories. There are many more ways to get people's interest if we dare to be bold and creative enough to use them. "Ho hum" is like striking a match to start a fire. Our "Ho Hum," then, should be passionately related to where we wish to take the listener in the body of the homily.

Second, keeping in mind that the listener always has a mind of his or her own, answer the following question early in the homily: "Why did you bring this up?" Answer the question without asking it, building a bridge from our thoughts to theirs, and from our thoughts to the Scriptures, and from our "Ho Hum" to the body of our text. Be brief, yet strong.

Third, "for instance..." means giving the listener clear, concrete examples and easily understandable cases. This implies that, as preacher, we know our listeners' wants, needs, and dreams. "Listeners like speakers who serve their 'for instances' as course dinners, not goulash!"[9] We must give examples that clearly illustrate and build a bridge to the listener's experience.

The more concrete and universal our examples or cases are, the more the congregation will identify with us and with the road down which we are leading them. For example, if you share a story about your grandmother, do not mention her name lest you risk having many members of our congregations go off on a tangent thinking about all the people they are reminded of by that name.

Let us not distract them from the relationship and how it relates to the Scriptures. "My grandmother" is more universal than "my grandmother, Bibi." The more universal the examples we use, the more the universal experiences of faith, hope, love, forgiveness, compassion, envy, jealousy, anger, frustration, etc., will connect with the people of different cultures, especially if we risk sharing our own struggles with those universal experiences.

Finally, the fourth principle: "SO WHAT!" What's the point? What does all this have to do with us, with my life here and now? Where do we go from here? Why should I leave the world I know to do what you say? We preachers must respond to the

---

9   ibid., pg. 12.

"So what!" challenge of the listener with "SO THIS...," giving the congregation some action response which they can accomplish. "Join! Contribute! Vote! Write! Telegraph! Buy! Boycott! Enlist! Investigate!"[10] Forgive! Come! Testify! Pray! Believe! These are examples of what we AND the listeners would do together. Never leave this step out.

I believe that we preachers want to bring meaning, coming from Good News, to the lives of the listeners. We must "destroy apathy, conquer discouragement, generate excitement, enthusiasm, electricity."[11] We must share the Pentecost experience that has driven us to say "YES" to Jesus' call to complete his work and BE his spokesperson. We must be interesting, challenging, and evoke an increase in faith, hope and love, because the Holy Spirit's fire makes us hammers and chisels in the hands of God, the Master Sculptor!

---

10   ibid., pg. 13.
11   Walter J. Burghardt, S. J., <u>Preaching: The Art and the Craft</u>, (New York: Paulist Press, 1987) pg. 1.

....

CHAPTER TWO

THE THREE QUESTIONS

"The purpose of life is to matter--to count, to stand for something, to have it make a difference that we have lived at all."[12]

I f we feel that we do not matter, count, or stand for something, or if we feel it has made no difference at all that we have lived, then we give in to the notion of being a "nobody." Jesus came so that the nobodies of His day and all days would know that they are God's somebodies. Our mission as preachers, should we choose to accept it, is the same: let people know they are important to us and to God, and loved just as they are. Doing so completes Christ's Mission.

To accomplish this, let us remember two things about our preaching: we are about God's work, and, we can influence people by our preaching. What an incredible responsibility and charge we have been given! Remembering these things will always keep us humble. God is the agenda-giver, not us. The medium or messenger and the message must both be Good News to the listener.

With these things in mind, let me share three questions that Fr. Joe Powers, S.J., had us ponder and discuss in our Christology class if we were to engage in Evangelizing. Joe said that if we answer "yes" to these three questions, we will be a successful evangelist:

---

12   Leo Buscaglia, Living, Loving, and Learning, (New York: Ballantine Books, a division of Random House, Inc., 1982) pg. 38.

1.) Does my homily (or presentation) come from my faith?
2.) Does it communicate my faith?
3.) Does it evoke or challenge my faith and that of the listener?

Joe also said that if we answer "no" to any <u>one</u> of these three questions, we should tear up our homily and start over.

Believe it or not, I had this happen to me the night before my sister's wedding. I was a deacon then, and I had completed the homily. I was practicing it out loud, taping it on a cassette player. (In taping the homily the voice you hear sounds different from how you hear your own voice.) Listening to my homily did not evoke my faith or challenge me as listener. I was not convinced by what I was sharing. (I not only preach to others, but also to myself.)

I tore it up and went to sleep that night. I had prayed to be guided by God in my sleep to find the words God wanted me to say to my sister and to our family and friends. By early next morning, I awoke and remembered a story. I used it as the "Ho Hum." It helped lay the foundation of the bridge to the Scriptures my sister had chosen for her Nuptial Mass. I had already prepared all week. This experience helped me become a better person because what I said to my sister and brother-in-law also applied to me in my life.

I have never been disappointed in the results when I ask myself these three questions prior to delivering a homily and have answered "yes" to them. Try asking yourself these questions and let God show you the way.

....

CHAPTER THREE

WHAT VOICE
ARE YOU IN?

For sacraments are not ends in themselves but means to an end. They are doors to the sacred, and so what really counts is not the doors themselves, but what lies beyond them. --Joseph Martos[13]

The function of the healer, the teacher, and the priest is to open the door. But, my friends, you must walk through it and discover what is on the other side. --Don How Li[14]

The risen, living Christ
calls us by name;
comes to the loneliness within us;
heals that which is wounded within us;
comforts that which grieves within us;
seeks for that which has dominion over us;
releases us from that which has dominion over us;
cleanses us of that which does not belong to us;
renews that which feels drained within us;
awakens that which is asleep in us;
names that which is still formless within us;
empowers that which is newborn within us;
consecrates and guides that which is strong within us;

---

13   Joseph Martos, <u>Doors to the Sacred</u>, (Garden City, New York: Image Books, 1982) pg. 130.
14   Molli Nickel, <u>Healing the Whole Person, the Whole Planet</u>, (Hillsboro, Oregon: Spirit Speaks, 1988) pg. 99.

restores us to this world which needs us;
reaches out in endless love to others through me.

--Flora Slosson Wuellner[15]

The preacher is the key in Christ's hand that unlocks the Doors to the Sacred which are the Sacraments. If we have not walked through them ourselves and discovered WHO is on the other side, how can we hope to help others do so? Preachers preach to others AND to themselves. Realizing this, we become like Christ who calls us by our name.... and asks us to do as He did.

Our preaching can be of service, like Christ in the words of Flora Wuellner's poem. The gift of story can serve, too. Who, on this earth, does not love a good story? What can consume a person, engulf a person, or mesmerize a person more than a well-woven story. Jesus was a masterful story-teller. In telling a story the preacher must heed the words of Christ: "Learn from me, for I am meek and humble of heart." (MT 11: 29) Jesus spoke with authority, spoke with His voice, and humbly let God's voice come forth. We must learn to do the same.

In my theological studies, I once took a "Storytelling and Preaching" class taught by Margie Brown, a woman who had suffered almost crippling effects from Muscular Dystrophy. She has taught herself to overcome its effects and to use what she had learned to become a wonderful teacher, preacher, and Evangelist. She did it as a one-person show in the genre of the clown.

On the first day of class she had us tell a story and then asked each of us: "What voice did you speak from?" All of us gave her the "what are you talking about" stare. We learned that there are three possible voices we can use when we tell a story and when we preach.

First is the "Once upon a Time" kind of voice. This is the voice used by our parents, grandparents, or guardians when they read stories to us. This is the voice in which we change our regular voice to narrate what is clearly not our experience, not our story, and hence we speak not in our true voice. We are not an integral part of the story. We are the teller of the story with no investment

---

15   Flora Slosson Wuellner, <u>Prayer, Fear, and our Powers</u>, (Nachville: Upper Room Books, 1989) pg. 120.

14

of our core-being in it because we tell it not as our own story.

Second is the "you will learn this or else" preachy, teachy, finger-pointing voice that few people enjoy hearing. Army generals, politicians and unfortunately, many preachers and ministers fall into this voice when they feel the need to push their agendas. This is the voice most parents use to discipline their children. All of us remember this voice, and tend to react negatively when reminded of those times. So, do most listeners.

Third is "MY own voice." This is the voice that speaks the truth without any hesitation or alteration. We are telling our story. The medium or messenger and the message are congruent. The messenger and the message are one. There is total investment because it comes from our inner authority, from the depths of our being, and it is obvious to the listener. This is the voice that convinces the listener that the preacher is speaking from experience.

In which voice do we usually preach? If we change our voices during the homily, are we doing so intentionally, with a purpose in mind? If we are aware of the voice we are using and use it to help speak the truth God is calling us to proclaim, then we are skillfully doing what we set out to do. How aware of our voice are we?

Is it possible to use our own voice to tell another's story? Yes, by placing ourselves in the story and letting ourselves experience the story. When we do this in praying with the Scriptures, we call it "contemplation," a stepping into the scene and seeing what we learn about God and ourselves in this process of prayer. Experiencing the story and letting it flow out of our own experience allows us to tell it as if it were our own.

As preachers we must become the protagonist in another's story as we do with Christ's. We must become part of the story. When we tell a story with total investment, we are using our own voice, and we will notice that the listener is riveted to our every word. The listener can't wait to hear how the story will relate to his or her life, or how it connects him or her with God. We can learn to tell another's story as our own!

When telling a story, the preacher may become emotional. There are times when emotions are permitted in the transmission of a story. (I know that some preachers disagree with me.) Emotions should be anticipated, resolved, and integrated within the teller prior to its delivery in a homily. If not, then the preacher is manipulating the congregation, seeking sympathy, which damages the relationship between preacher and listener, and diminishes the impact of God's Word. The medium or messenger and the message are not congruent. The messenger and the message are obviously not one.

If we are telling the story and an emotion comes naturally, and at a point calling for it, we risk showing our vulnerability before the people to whom we preach. This shows the listeners that the preacher trusts them and is with them. They feel understood and so appreciate when the preacher honors them by risking being as vulnerable as they are.

A preacher shouldn't use the homily just to draw given emotional responses from the people. In African-American communities there are often responses like "Amen!" or "Alleluia!" I am not talking about these responses. I am talking about trying to elicit feelings like pity, anger, revenge. Doing this betrays the preacher's relationship with them and betrays the Good News, too.

Nevertheless, the intimacy between the preacher and the people can elicit an emotional response. There are times when I, in telling a story, become so caught up by the story and so caught up in the listener's response to the story, that I am moved, even to tears. Preachers, give yourself permission to feel the effects of your own words, and God's Word, if they are delivered authentically.

If authentic, this vulnerability will permit the listeners to feel as well. This gives them permission to join with us instead of feeling sorry for us. They will discover their truth about the connection of their story to yours and to Christ's. If our emotions come from our authentic voice, fear not. If they do not come from our authentic voice, DO NOT tell that particular story in the homily.

Our voice betrays the amount of investment we preachers have with the story we are telling and with the homily we are delivering. If we never speak in our own voice, then we will never be telling our story nor Christ's story in our own. If you use it, they will hear!

May we always preach from our own true voice and tell Christ's story as our own story so that others may become part of THE STORY of God's Presence and Love, of God's Good News.

CHAPTER FOUR

KNOW YOUR AUDIENCE

"To preach is to shout a whisper. What does it mean...? It means to speak boldly and clearly, but to trust the Word as the sower trusts the seed to carry its own future in itself and make its own way to the heart. It means to proclaim what we have heard, being true to the received tradition, but being careful to frame it in the context of the listeners... The Bread of Life is broken and offered, but the hearer must be allowed to chew for oneself....shouting a whisper certainly means respecting the listener's resistance to the message."[16]

Respecting the listener's resistance to a message is an awesome charge. It implies that our efforts must stand on their own because we have no control over whether the listener will truly listen and be ready to accept the challenge of a homily that has been well planned and delivered. The preacher must humbly recognize that most of the listeners think differently from the preacher.

If the reader is familiar with Personality Typing, such as the writings of David Kiersey and Marilyn Bates[17] on the findings of Drs. Isabel Myers and Katheryn Briggs, then you know that most people process reality in ways unlike that of the preacher. If you are not familiar with Personality Typing, let me summarize and clarify.

---

16 Fred B. Craddock, <u>Preaching</u>, (Nashville: Abingdon Press, 1985) p. 64.
17 They wrote: <u>Please Understand Me</u>, (Del Mar: Promethius Nemesis Book Company, 1984

According to Isabel Myers and Kathryn Briggs, humans tend to perceive in one of two ways: through sensation or intuition. The difference between them is the source of most miscommunication and arguments. The difference between them can keep people apart and can cause misunderstandings.

The "sensate" type wants facts: the more facts, the more details, the better. The "sensate" knows through life's experiences. He or she enjoys reading or hearing about personal histories. The "sensate" wants to know the details of the other's experiences. He or she learns through "noticing." Before a "sensate" type solves a problem, he or she needs every fact AND a step by step process they can follow in order to understand the problem and find a solution.

The "intuitive" type, on the other hand, seldom notices details. He or she tends to scan situations based upon prior experiences. Imagery and ideas attract the "intuitive" type. The "intuitive" learns more through "seeing," through ideas. He or she loves metaphors. He or she enjoys fiction and fantasy. Facts are fine if they add to the fantastic. The possible excites the "intuitive" type. The "intuitive" does not solve a problem in a step-by-step process, but rather by a knowing that grasps the solution immediately, almost like a spark.

It is important to note that neither way of processing reality is better than the other. They are just different. Both ways are God-given. Both are necessary to help each other know more deeply the whole of creation, the whole of our God (to the extent possible). Knowing the difference and knowing that people in the congregation think and process differently from you, the preacher, can help the preacher become a more effective communicator of God's truth.

According to Kiersey and Bates, seventy-five percent of the general population tends to be a sensate preference, while twenty-five percent are intuitive. I am an "intuitive." That means that three out of every four people in the congregation are "sensates," more in need of facts and step-by-step descriptions than I do. "Intuitives" do not need these because they see the solution or the point directly.

"Sensate" and "intuitive" are but two of the many factors that make the combinations of people in the congregation different from the preacher. For example, I am also an extrovert, a person who thinks out loud and who is energized by a crowd of people. Introverts need time alone to think and reflect, and they are de-energized by large groups of people. They prefer a one-on-one relationship to mixing with a crowd.

I am also a feeler, one who makes decisions based on my gut feelings, as opposed to a thinker, who makes decisions based more on logic and rules or principles. And finally, I am a perceiver, a person who is open to the possibilities, and who feels encumbered by schedules or deadlines. Others are judgers, who work on one idea at a time, who need the closure of schedules and deadlines.

There are many combinations of the above types. Whatever the combination, the preacher is always in the minority. At least 52% of the congregation processes differently from the preacher. My type: Extrovert, Intuitive, Feeler, and Perceiver, makes up 12% of the population. Hence, seven of eight people process reality differently from how I do.

What can I do, then, as an intuitive, in order to reach the majority? I must combine the metaphoric language of possibilities with bridge sentences that help the "sensate" person understand the connections that I make naturally without the need of step-by-step processes. If I skip steps, or if I jump from story to story or example to example without showing the connection, I risk losing the sensate listener. I must use concrete, logically connected examples to help the sensates learn and understand.

The "sensate" preacher must be careful not to over-do details. Ask yourself if details are necessary to make your points. Why? Because "intuitive" types can become easily bored with fact and detail, or they can become distracted by the details and go off on tangents that can consume their thought. "Intuitive" listeners will think to themselves, "Bring us home preacher!" because they already see where the "sensate" preacher is going. They can get lost in the forest of details and lose the point.

How do you learn? Are you aware of how you process reality? Are you aware of how the listener learns and processes? We preachers must study and understand how our preaching style communicates our faith to the listener and evokes or challenges our faith and the faith of the listener.

Have a person who thinks differently from you listen to your homily prior to its delivery. Have others evaluate it honestly after it is delivered. Tape and listen to yourself. These aids will help you learn about yourself and the listener.

We must know our strengths and preach from them. We must know our weaknesses and overcome them by bridging the communicated word to the ability of the listener to "hear." This is what it means to frame the homily in the context of the listener.

I love to tell stories and to let the stories tell themselves. I also love to use metaphors and similes when I preach. I enjoy stringing together a series of stories, whose connections to each other are obvious to the "intuitive" listener. On the other hand, since the majority of the people are "sensate" listeners, I know they need a step-by-step process in order to "see" or understand the connections.

For example, I once gave a homily on the Transfiguration in a homiletics class. I used the story of the sculptor, which I shared at the beginning of this book, to begin the homily. I then told a story about my encounter with Michaelangelo's Pietá in Rome. Finally, I told a story about my being with a mother in the hospital who was holding her dying son. I wanted to illustrate the transfigurations which occur in all of our lives. I thought the stories were obviously connected to each other. The mystery of God is in the heart of the sculptor who recognizes God in the marble. The mystery of the awesome relationship between Mary and Jesus after the crucifixion, was parallel to the mother and son at the hospital. I did not connect the stories, I just shared them one by one.

I didn't use bridge sentences describing how each story led into the other and how they were connected. The eleven "sensate" listeners said to me: "The stories were great, but what's the point?" The three "intuitive" listeners in the class were moved. I was humbled to learn I had missed the mark with most of my classmates.

May we always show humility by respecting the listener's way of hearing. May we frame our word pictures in ways that invite the listener to "come and see." Let us also remember that the listener wants to find the reality beyond the door to the Sacred through our homily, and wants us to move him or her to enter the door in doing so. They want us to succeed! Let us truly know our audience.

CHAPTER FIVE

GET HELP IN PREPARING

Can you say that, like St. Ignatius, you have truly encountered the living and true God? Can you say that you know God Himself, not simply human words that describe Him? If you cannot, I dare not conclude that you are an unproductive preacher; for the same God who "is able from these stones to raise up children of Abraham" (MT 3:9) can use the most sere of sermons to move the obdurate heart. But do I say that if you know only a theology of God, not the God of theology, you will not be the preacher our world desperately needs.[18]

1.) <u>LITURGY PLANNING</u>

L et me share some suggestions for encountering the living and true God in ways not often available in parishes or schools. Nine years ago, I offered a class on the Mass to any who would come and learn. I felt that if people learned about the Mass, its history, its development, its possibilities for encountering God in their lives and in liturgy, then they would jump at the chance to evaluate, each week, what we, as a parish, were offering, including the homily.

I was right. Since May of 1991, between twelve and forty parishioners have gathered each Monday evening. We gather first to evaluate the Eucharist from the point of view of Mass ministry:

---

18   Walter Burghardt, S.J., <u>Preaching: The Art and the Craft</u>, (New York: Paulist Press, 1987) p. 60-61.

i.e. Hospitality, Presiding, Lectoring, Eucharistic Ministry, and the Music. Then, we evaluate the Homily in the presence of the Preacher.

I had to help them become comfortable critiquing the preacher, because people don't want to "hurt the preacher's feelings." I told them: "start with the theme that was set last week and share how the preacher reached or missed the mark." It takes humility to overcome the fear of being critiqued. It takes humility to overcome the fear of critiquing a person's work in the person's presence. When done with kindness and charity, grace happens.

Immediately following the evaluation, which takes about fifteen minutes, the lay people read aloud the Scripture passages for the coming Sunday. The leader, who is either the priest scheduled to preside the following Sunday, or the deacon or a lay person, then asks those present: "Are there any words or phrases of impact? Could you share them first without comment?" What we are doing is *Lectio Divina* in a group.

We come up with a list of five to eight words or phrases that impacted them, and examine them, one-by-one, asking the person who spoke up to share what impacted them. During this sharing, many questions and issues are raised, and many faith-moments surface. The environment of inquiring can lead them to ask theological or moral questions of the priest or deacon that they have never been able to ask before. What a teachable moment!

This offers a great opportunity for the preacher to help the people learn what we have all learned through our own study, reflection and life. What teachable moments these have become for both the preacher and the people at Christ the King! The preacher "hears" the stories of those who represent the hopes, dreams, fears and joys of the greater worshipping community, and it gives the people a chance to hear the preacher share outside the liturgical setting. We all become both teachers and students of the Word.

Once this hour-long process has been completed, the leader asks: "From what has been shared, can we come up with a powerful and provocative theme for Sunday in the form of a short question, declaration, or phrase?" Themes are shared and then we pause, in silence, to let the Spirit move a person to speak out with authority. Trust in the Holy Spirit is important. The Spirit has never failed us. The "right" theme for that Sunday always surfaces by God's grace.

The preacher, if he or she takes notes, now has the comments and stories of the people, the Scriptures, the Commentaries to which he or she subscribes, one's own story, books and homily helps with stories to pray over, reflect on, and craft into a homily. The preacher sees the people's need to hear the preacher's own story interwoven with theirs and Christ's. The preacher can observe the listener's need to know that one is not alone in one's struggles, joys, sorrows and victories, and that one has made a difference that one shared at all. A listening preacher can't help but become a better preacher.

If the reader is entertaining the thought that this process simply becomes a popularity contest to see which neat theme is selected, let me tell you that the people are thirsting for the preacher to focus and deal with the problems of life in relation to God. People want to hear how we, as preachers, deal with frustration, anguish, joy, sorrow, forgiveness, the absence or the presence of God. They want to know that we are walking with them and that we know what they are going through. They want to know how we find God in our life's struggles and how to find God in their own struggles.

They want to know where the preacher is in all this, where GOD is in all this, and where THEY stand in what we call reality. That is why the "SO WHAT" is so important. Preacher, challenge yourself; challenge the people of God!

2.) <u>USE STORIES</u>

Many times it is the "Ho Hum" which is the key to the door of the people's thought patterns. Be creative with your "HO HUMS." You can use stories in the beginning as a "Ho Hum." Use stories whenever you can to illustrate points and build bridges for the people to connect Christ's story with their own.

I once used the "Mission Impossible" theme on Mission Sunday. I taped my own voice to deliver the tune and the story and played it through our sound system, and then continued to share what I had prepared. Other times I have used the refrain of a song or poem. I have even "become" the protagonist in the Gospel scene. The people will be with you; they will learn; they will be moved to act; they will grow with you in the Lord.

Use stories in your "FOR INSTANCE," or even at the end as a "SO WHAT." No matter where you place the story, people will better remember the themes of your homilies because they remember the stories you used.

3.) GET A HOMILY PARTNER

We, as preachers, need to find a person or group with whom to test the homily. Doing so, we will be informed as to whether or not what we wish to accomplish is actually being accomplished. Our homily partners can expose blind spots and verbosity. They can suggest how better to reinforce a powerful idea. This process, along with listening to our own "taped" version, helps keep us humble and honest with ourselves. Instead of hanging our heads when our friend or colleague says: "It is missing something" or "This is not one of your best," let us take it as a challenge to know ourselves and God more intimately and to go back and rewrite. We will not regret it.

I can't stress enough how this has helped me to overcome my weaknesses by listening to them being exposed in a safe and instructive setting. It has helped me become more aware of my own tendency to use theological or churchy language when I preach.

Theological terms and churchy terms are seldom understood by the people. They are certainly not understood by non-Catholics or non-Christians who might be present. Avoid them if you can. It is better to use other, more universally understood words to explain the same idea. After all, are we not about bringing all people closer to God? Don't risk losing them over jargon.

4.) K.I.S.S. SCHOOL OF HOMILETICS

How often have I seen people look strangely at the preacher who uses big words, jargon words, words that the average person does not see and can't possibly understand unless they have studied philosophy or theology. KEEP IT SIMPLE STUPID! I belong to the K.I.S.S. schools of life and of preaching.

We don't realize how much our heads can separate us from the people! "I give you praise, Father, for although you have hidden these things from the wise and the learned, you have revealed them to the merest children."(MT 11:25b) That verse moved me in philosophy studies, and it still moves me. It makes me ask: How can I bring my knowledge and insights to the people? and then to translate my answer into the people's language.

What helps me to do this is to pretend that everyone in the congregation is a non-believer. (There is a bit of a non-believer in all of us.) I ask myself, "How would I say what I want to say to someone who does not know Christ?" If I use theological or church-related terms, those people will not understand. Those words are explained in the R.C.I.A (Rite of Christian Initiation of Adults) process, where candidates learn about the faith, preparing for baptism into the Church. Do not use Church jargon in a homily.

God-talk is analogous. Our metaphors, similes and stories must use language anyone, especially children, can understand and respond to. If we use a big word, explain them as we go. Let us not risk losing people because they don't understand us.

At one of our high schools one preached using words that I would have needed a dictionary to understand, let alone follow. I went to him, as a fellow Jesuit, and asked why he had used words that most of the congregation couldn't possibly know? His answer: "To show them the vocabulary they need to survive college." I asked: "But what about the Word of God? What about the listener?"

5.) <u>MAKE THE LENGTH 10 MINUTES or LESS</u>

I have heard, "If you haven't struck oil in three minutes, quit boring." I have heard the rules of thumb that homilies should be seven to ten minutes in length. If a homily or sermon is badly composed, even three minutes is too long. If a homily is well composed, the homilist will always give the listener the desire to hear more. The listener will experience a sadness that it has ended.

Some parishes have circumstances that dictate just how long one can preach. Many have Masses one right after the other on the hour or half-hour. Don't let worrying about the length of the homily spoil the moment.[19] However, we must know that we have

---

19 I use New York 14 Font. Each typed Page is 4 minutes in delivery. That is my gauge.

all been "programmed" to have a 10-minute attention span due to Radio/TV's commercial message every 10 minutes. Hence, listeners are attentive for 10 minutes!

There are many ways to bring the message and the Liturgy to the people within the time-limits dictated by the pastoral situation. The presider can instruct the choir to sing fewer verses, or one can use a different Eucharistic prayer, and/or increase the number of Eucharistic Ministers. In my former parish we spread out the Mass times to better serve the varieties of cultures present at Christ the King.[20] At Most Holy Trinity, I had to discipline myself so that we finish Mass in an hour, because we had seven Masses every Sunday.

Stories take time to tell. Good, life-centered stories take time to relate them to the Scriptures. When well told, no one will ever look at his or her watch. Connect the story to the Scriptures, and give concrete, relevant examples, and you will keep the attention of even the smallest child. Preach to the child, and the child in the adult listens. Preach to the adult and you've lost the child.

6.) <u>KEEP TRACK OF WHEN & WITH WHOM YOU'VE PREACHED</u>

I always keep track of which Masses or services, which language groups, and which congregations I use a particular story with. I have never used the same story more than once with a particular congregation. I also have every homily I have ever delivered on my computer disc and in hard copy, both for personal reference and for ideas for a new homily on future Sundays.

---

20   The 7:00 and 8:30 AM Masses are in English. Both are Gospel Masses with Gospel choirs. The next two Masses, in Spanish are at 11:00 AM and 1:00 PM Mass in Spanish. We value both cultural differences in worship and having the time to share table fellowship in the hall after Mass.

CHAPTER SIX

CONCLUDING REMARKS

We have seen a simple structure for the homily that uses the four rules of "public speaking as listeners like it." We have seen three questions to test the preacher's passion and to see if we have made ourselves instruments of God's Word. We have learned how to ask ourselves which voice we are using to preach. We have seen some insights into the different personality types that exist in the congregation, and how to reflect upon bridging the gap between preachers and listeners. Finally, we have seen some practical suggestions that might help us become better at the marvelous craft and art we call Preaching.

Let me now share homilies for the entire Year C, since the Catholic Lectionary is a 3-year that exposes the faithful to the 4 Gospels in 3 years. Note how stories are used to bring the message of Christ's love for us home to rest.

At the end, I will share with you a Bibliography of books and story sources. I hope you find them as helpful as I have in the shaping and refining of your homiletic skills. God bless you all.

HOMILIES

1st in ADVENT: Wait, the best is yet to come!

The word Advent means "come to." We await Christ, Jesus Christ, coming to earth, to our human condition, taking it on and showing us how to live it to its fullest. But, why? Why would God become incarnate and let one's self be born poor, suffer, and eventually die in a gruesome manner? Let me share some thoughts to prepare us for a fruitful Advent. Martin Luther King, Jr., once said:

"The true neighbor risks one's position, one's prestige, and even one's life for the welfare of others. In dangerous... and hazardous pathways, one will lift some bruised, beaten brother/sister to a higher and more noble life."

Another person once shared:

"Dr. Keith Phillips, founder of World Impact, tried to minister to an L.A. ghetto, Watts by commuting from upper-class Woodlawn. He came to see how futile it was to try. He applied for public housing and as raised his family in inner-city Watts. Dr. Phillips understood that to impact a ghetto, to make a difference, you must be willing to live in the ghetto." (Paraphrased from "A Mountain too high to Climb," Dynamic Preaching, 1995, pg. 2)

Drs. King & Phillips' touch on why Jesus had to come to earth. The Trinity realizes what Dr. King and Keith Phillips realized: to impact their creation, to make a difference, we must be willing to live in the world, to be a true neighbor. The Trinity saw that the earth and its inhabitants had taken a path toward selfishness and a lack of respect for the giftedness that we are for each other. So men and women we call prophets like Jeremiah, Martin, or Keith were sent redirect us. When it didn't work, someone greater was needed. The Trinity decides to send Jesus as the 1st reading says: "to instruct us in God's ways and walk in God's paths," for the best is yet to come.

Has Jesus really made a difference; does he impact in our lives? If not, it is not too late to let the miracle of the incarnation, soak us all the way to our bones. Are we prepared to welcome him in a new way this Christmas? Are we prepared for Jesus Christ to change our lives forever? That's why we have Advent. The best to come.

Kids, Jesus is alive and well in your parents, catechists, teachers and coaches. How do we know? He said, "I will be with you always." The question remains, do you believe this or not. If so, you will listen and learn your lessons well. If not, you will sell your soul to the loudest.

Parents, Jesus is alive and well in your children. Jesus said, "from the mouth of babes comes the wisdom of God." They were sent to teach you how to raise children. Do you believe this or not? If so, you will listen and learn how to come out of yourself. If not, you will lose them.

Parish, Jesus is alive and well all around you. How do we know? Jesus said, "Where 2 or 3 gather in my name, there I am among them." In fact, we Catholics believe he is present in the assembly, in the Word, in the priest, the Bread and Wine of life, and in well played music. Do we live our lives believing this or not? If so, we will leave here ready to live our Mission Statement. If not, we'll sell our souls to be the hypocrites Jesus always confronted in the Gospels.

Jesus wants to impact us. He wants to see the impact by seeing our swords beaten into plowshares, our weapons of war turned into the utensils of feeding a hungry, love-starved world. He wants to see our families divided by the ism's and the addictions of the world, healed forever. He wants all grudges to end, leading to a lasting peace.

Jesus wants to see the impact of ending gang-banging, discrimination, machismo, racism, sexism, gender-ism, age-ism, alcoholism, drugs, sex, food, child, spouse, or parental abuse, work-aholism, and consumerism. He wants to see the presence of the fruits of the Holy Spirit in us: love, peace, patience, self-control, kindness, gentleness, faithfulness, & generosity. Do we show we have them? If not, it's not too late to give in.

May we understand as Jesus did. May we step into the world of others and live with them so that we can change each other. Let Christ change us into the best, for our best is yet to come.

2nd in ADVENT: Pause, and let yourself be changed!

A few years ago a friend of mine had me read a tiny, but significant book: *The Pause*. The title so intrigued me, I opened it and read on.

It was the story about a boss who received a bag filled with wrapped boxes. It was the week of Christmas, and the boxes were from the staff. An assistant said, "Go ahead and open them." So he did. One by one he opened boxes containing what his staff knew he'd like: light rock CD's, a fountain pen, a watch with a stop-start button.

Then he opened a beautifully wrapped box that had all kinds of cotton inside, and nothing else. He just stared. His assistant smiled at his quizzical look and said, "What are you thinking?" Since he said nothing, she chimed in, "It's the gift of a pause. You're so busy about many things, I felt you needed to pause and think, even for just a moment. See? It worked."

The period between Thanksgiving and Christmas has become a frantic-paced, commercialized time filled with shoulds. We should do this, get this, accomplish this, buy this. However, the only real "should" is: to pause and reflect on the reason for the season: Jesus Christ.

The Church's wisdom has given us the gift of that pause. It's called: Advent. We're asked to pause and think about what Christ's birth meant to his people, what it means to us now, what his promise of returning might do to our thinking and thus, our lives?

John the Baptist said, "Prepare ye the way of the Lord." He wanted his people to repent, that is, to look at life in a new way by pushing the pause-button, and letting themselves be changed by that new look, by that pause. He asks us to look at life as Robert Kennedy did: "Some people look at the world as it is and ask 'Why?' I dream dreams that never were, and ask 'Why not?'" John is asking us to see how Jesus, our hero, did this. What makes him our hero? Heroes make a difference. Jesus made a difference, so much so that here we are 2000 years later.

Heroes and she-roes change the world around them. Has Christ changed ours? If so, how do we show it and how do we witness to it? Are we helping to make straight God's paths? Are we trying to help people fill-in the valleys of their hearts with the love and presence of God, replacing their addictions or compulsions with Christ? Are we the voice of God in their wilderness of loss, pain, and isolation?

We're called to pause and ask and answer the question, "How do I want to be remembered by my loved ones, by God, and by future generations, when I die?" Then ask: "Am I living this way right now? If so, we'll become the she-roes and heroes we were created to be.

CNN's program to honor real-life heroes had 2 of them forced to pause and think about their lives and those of others in the world. One paused with the question of how to make a difference for children who die due to contaminated water. That pause changed him, and gives his time to ending this tragedy, one town at a time.

The other had his legs amputated at age 8 by the propeller of his parents' boat. Never complaining, he saw the difficulties in getting and affording the prosthetics he needed for a more normal life. At age 11 he decided to fund-raise so other children like him would never go without the prosthetics they need. 10 years later he's made a difference. His foundation disperses $1/2 million a year to make that happen.

Advent is a time to pause, listen to John's message of repentance, and let our hearts be stirred into becoming heroic messengers of God's Good News to a world surrounded by bad news. If we take advantage of this gift, if we pause and let ourselves be stirred to act by it, we'll convert our hearts into mangers where Christ will come to us and to others once more. Now, isn't that worth pausing for?

3rd in ADVENT: Are we willing to change?

What a personality John must have been! Imagine people from all over coming to hear his message of repentance, that is, of looking again at life and letting oneself be changed by that look! They came to him with, "What must I do?" They begged for homework! John knew his people well enough to assign them the right kind of homework, one that would reward their work of repentance.

For those of us wondering "what's God's will for us?," we can't go wrong by focusing on what leads to Social Justice. Social Justice, social right-relationship, is a triangle. One point of the triangle is Advocacy, a 2nd is Direct Service and the 3rd, Empowerment. Few of us are good at all 3. However, God is calling us just as we are to <u>do</u> at least one of them.

Perhaps you like to serve the poor directly: feeding them, clothing them, housing them. Perhaps you like being the voice of the voiceless, or defending the defenseless. You can speak for them through Community Organizing. Join with organizations like PACT or the Interfaith Council for Economic and Social Justice. Finally, you might be good at helping people fend for themselves. Our employment center, our counseling center, our resource or housing center is for you. Or, perhaps you can help our principal market our schools, the best-kept secrets in our area.

John the Baptist helped his people understand what to do by saying what St. Ignatius tells us Jesuits to do when we find our way of doing things turning out badly: *Agere Contra,* "Do the opposite." John told those who felt like changing due to his preaching, to change by doing the opposite of what they had been doing.

So I've been asking myself, if President Obamma, Congress, our city officials and business leaders were to ask John the same question today, what would John's answer be? He'd say, "You who espouse family values, reform your Immigration policy to keep families together."

"You, who duped the poor or the unsuspecting into signing mortgages that were wrong to be offered, pay back what you stole and modify the loans to keep families in their houses. You, who use the law to write "fine-print" contracts, write contracts that are easy to understand and follow. You, who consider yourselves the police of the world, stop bullying and find a way to peace. You, who are helping to destroy God's mother earth, sign the World Environment Summit accords, and stop global-warming."

We can go on, but you get the point! These admonitions are meant for us all, because how we speak out or not, shows whether we're part of the problem or part of the solution. Advent is a time to consider being part of the solutions to human problems.

Advent is time to ask ourselves, "What must I do to be a better person in 2015?" Once we identify the areas to be improved, we must ask for the grace to change what we can change. And, trusting we've received the grace we asked for, act on it. Don't let it be returned like the gifts we don't like. Real repentance, the process of re-looking at life and letting ourselves be changed by that re-look, will act. Otherwise we'll be like one who always says "I'm sorry," after doing wrong, and then goes on repeating the same wrong. There's no real sorrow, only a bad habit.

We heard Paul say, "Rejoice in the Lord always, again I say rejoice. Your kindness should be known to all. The Lord is near." (Phil 4:4-5) That's the message behind the pink Advent-candle and vestments. Today is Gaudete Sunday, meaning Rejoicing Sunday. It is an attempt to keep us hopeful while we prepare our hearts to be mangers for Christ.

When we come to communion today, let our hands become a manger for the host, symbolic of converting our hearts into mangers for Christ, too. May we leave here resolved to do what John the Baptist or Christ has told us to do: change for the better.

Eduardo A. Samaniego, S.J.

4th in ADVENT: Buns are to be enjoyed!

Have you ever heard, "She has a bun in the oven?" It's a way of saying a woman is pregnant. Now, did you know that <u>Bethlehem</u> literally means, "House of Bread?" How totally symbolic is the Nativity Story! Jesus, the Bread of Life, is taken as a "bun in the oven" to Bethlehem, the House of Bread, then is born and put into a feeding trough, called a manger. Jesus is born into poverty to feed us with God's love.

The angel Gabriel, God's messenger, is sent to 2 families to announce that each will soon have a bun-in-the-oven, and give birth to sons that would change the course of history, and so feed peoples ever since with the love and forgiveness of God. It was good news to Zechariah and to Mary. Even though shocked, they both gave themselves to it.

Our 4th Sunday in Advent makes us ponder the prophetic message that God-with-us will elevate the poor and humble the rich. "Blessed are you who believed" said Elizabeth to Mary, and she says it to us. We're here because we believe in the mystery of God, whose name, Emmanuel, or God-with-us. When we believe as Mary did, great things happen. Listen to a mother's story:

Despite all the stories of giving birth, and the words of wisdom from so-called "experts," nothing had prepared me for the joy of the experience to come. At 26 I was very fortunate of having, what you'd call, an "easy, good natured baby!" I could take her to a restaurant or to friends. She'd sit, play, or color in her coloring books, entertaining herself, and always played well with others. As she grew a little older, she'd enjoy sitting with her dad and me, and listen to our conversations about when she was a little baby, in awe and with curious eyes!

When Elizabeth said to Mary: "Blessed are you ... and blessed is the fruit of your womb...Blessed are you who believed," it reflects to me, that we as mothers, and all parents, are blessed with a special bond and joy for our children, and that we are as special as Elizabeth, who wondered how the Lord's mother would come to her.

34

My daughter has grown into a fine, compassionate woman, who now shares with me <u>her</u> wisdom and knowledge! Needless to say, I'm truly a blessed and proud mother as I look forward to continue to share with her, this journey of faith, hope and love.

I love to watch 2 mothers, or soon-to-be mothers talking. They not only glow because of their babies, they glow because they're sharing a secret, and the wisdom that motherhood brings. They change before our eyes. Blessed are you who believe.

We get a glimpse of this in the Gospel. Mary & Elizabeth are giddy with the knowledge that they're mothers. Filled with the Holy Spirit, both know they're about to change history. Blessed are you who believe.

God informs those who are filled with the Holy Spirit with things that need to be shared boldly with others. Once shared, fear is defeated. Elizabeth, filled with the Holy Spirit, cries out in a loud voice: "Blessed are you among women, and blessed is the fruit of your womb." (Lk 1:42) Mary, filled with the Holy Spirit, proclaims: The Magnificat: "My soul proclaims the greatness of the Lord and my spirit rejoices in God, my savior." In it she proclaims God's greatness over those considered great by society. Blessed are you who believe.

I'm here to tell you that today these words have been fulfilled in your hearing. Holy is God's name. We've all received the Holy Spirit and, if we cooperate with Her as Mary and Elizabeth did, then great things will happen and we'll make a difference that we have lived at all. Blessed are you who believe.

Are you ready for Jesus' coming? Are you ready for the bun in the oven of your heart to go out to tell the world how good God is in your own Magnificat? Are you ready to be bold proclaimers of what God has done and is doing in your lives right now? Then let's celebrate for Blessed are we who believe, and blessed is the fruit of our Faith!

CHRISTMAS EVE:
Christ is King of the upside-down and inside-out.

4 weeks ago we celebrated Christ our King, and then began the Advent trek toward repeating his story from the beginning, from his birth. It's like reading a book we've read many times or seeing a movie we've watched over and over. I would like to begin my last Christmas homily with you by telling you what kind of King Christ really was and is: he is the king of the upside-down and inside-out. How so?

Mary, the revolutionary, shared in her Magnificat all you need to know about upside-down and inside-out. "My soul magnifies the Lord and my spirit rejoices in God my Savior." Why? "Because the mighty has done great things for a nobody in society, me, who is not an emperor, a president, or rich and powerful. "He has scattered the proud and cast down the mighty," but has lifted up the nobodies of today. "God has filled the hungry with good things, and the rich God has sent away empty." How inside-out of God to change society's categories of insiders and outsiders, don't you think? Mary didn't share our American values. Hers are upside-down and inside-out from ours.

Jesus, the son of a poor, working-class family, was born in a cave, because there was no room in the inns of his day, and so his 1st bed was a box filled with animal's food, hay. In 3 days we will read about how our Holy Family became refugees, emigrating to another country to escape the danger that lurked behind the jealousy of the local king. Imagine how they'd be treated here in the USA if they had emigrated today!

These are not the normal thoughts about Christmas and its spirit, but they are the truth, and the truth will set us free from false gods and false notions of discipleship and apostleship. We must see that Jesus had enemies even before his birth. How upside-down then his message: "love your enemies, do good to those who harm you!" The Middle East, Ireland, Africa, Latin America, and our own country must practice this.

We've all heard "practice makes perfect." Bishop Ken Utener said it doesn't! "Practice makes permanent!" That's why we need to practice the perfect, to make it permanent. Imagine a permanent peace on earth! It can come only when we practice peace in ourselves, our family, our neighborhood, our country, and then abroad.

Jesus said the 1st would be last and the last 1st. Sounds upside-down and inside-out to me! Tell that to the Donald Trumps and Warren Buffets and their <u>wanna-be</u> disciples! The rich say, "to the strong go the spoils, blessed are the rich, who have found God's favor." Jesus counters with, "Blessed are the poor, for theirs is the kingdom of heaven" and "the meek shall inherit the earth!" Inside-out! No?

We're becoming a society of <u>need-to-haves</u>, and not <u>need-to-be</u> as Christ calls us to be. We need <u>not</u> do more but <u>be more</u> like Christ.

So, what does this have to do with celebrating Christmas here? Everything! Kids, do you know that 12 million children go to bed hungry in the US alone? Imagine yourself hungry every night. What can you do about this? Be creative! We do it to Jesus when we feed them.

Parents, be educators, examples, and doers of God's will, wrapped up in living in the way you want God and your loved ones to remember you. We've been sold a bill of goods that says that happiness is about having! It is not! Happiness is about who we are, whose we are, and for whom we were given this gift of life. We are humans belonging to Christ so that we can serve Christ in the least of his kingdom.

Christmas in the Bible is not Christmas in the Mall. The manger scene is not about a holy-card, Kodak-moment in history, but about the Bread of life, being born in Bethlehem, the House of Bread, feeding us with God's love so that we, in turn, leave here today ready to feed people who are starving to know God has not forgotten or forsaken them. Be that Bread and you will truly be someone's upside-down cake of life!

CHRISTMAS DAY: Parents of all

We have wonderful memories of Christmases, don't we? They're memorable because of the people, right? And the most joyous ones had children around.

There was once a great chief who was very, very proud. He loved to go about the village and boast of his greatness. "There is no one greater than I," he would say. Of course, everyone would roll their eyes.

One day, a wise old woman in the tribe had enough and came up to the chief and said, "I know one who is truly great, and he isn't you." "What! Who is greater than I? No one!" She answered his boast with, "Come to my house tomorrow at high noon, and I will introduce you to the great one." "OK, I will be there. We'll see who is the greatest!"

The chief went home and went to bed early so as to be well rested and strong for the encounter. In the morning he had a good breakfast, exercised, cleaned up and put on his finest clothing. While he did so, he thought about all the things he did better than everyone else in the tribe. "How can anyone be greater than I?" He repeated that thought all the rest of the morning and even as he walked up to the woman's door. She was ready for him and invited the chief inside. He immediately noticed how well kept the house was, and that there was an infant crawling on the floor to his right. "Ok, ok, where is this great chief you blabbed on about?"

Pointing to the child she said, "This is the great one I spoke of." Un-amused, he asked, "What do you mean? You're joking, right?" His voice became louder with every word, and the baby, frightened by his loudness, began to cry. Embarrassed by it all, the chief got down on his hands and knees, pulled a feather from his headdress, and began to gently stroke the child's cheek. He took his medicine bag and held it up to the child's nose. Nothing worked. He then took off his necklace of beads and shook them to distract the child. Sure enough, it calmed down and began to listen and watched with a smile.

"You see," said the woman, "even you, great chief, had to stop talking to take care of the baby. A baby is great because our creator planned it so. The creator did not make you great so that you can brag about your greatness. The creator made you great so that you could help those who aren't as strong as you." no one ever heard him brag again.

(Paraphrased from "The Baby Leapt," Dynamic Preaching, Vol. XXI, No. 4, Oct.-Dec., 2006, pg. 85)

How interesting that our God would choose to come into the world as a helpless babe! God's people were stiff-necked, disobedient, selfish, mean, even violent. It sounds a lot like many people today, doesn't it? With great wisdom, God chose to come among us as a child of a poor, insignificant couple, in an insignificant town, so that we could all stop talking and to stop using and abusing each other long enough to pay attention to the most significant of births.

It is God's way of saying, "Shut up and take notice for just one moment!" Who here does not have one's being softened by an infant's presence? Why? Because that's how God wired us. So, have you ever thought that we're all that size in God's eyes? God so loved us, Jesus was sent to show us and tell us how much we are loved. But God knew we'd need to have our attention diverted from me-ness to other-ness. Nothing does it better than to have a child in our midst. A child is God-with-us.

Today I'd like to divert you to the fact our child was born in Bethlehem, a town whose name means "House of Bread." He was placed in a manger, which is really a feeding trough. And Jesus is destined to be the Bread of Life. So today, as we ponder the reality of God becoming one of us to show us how God loves the idea of us, let us be nursed into becoming true apostles, sent to stop bragging, stop fixating on ourselves, and start proclaiming what God has done for us, more so with our lives than our lips.

We've made the Christ-children of the world so afraid that he's crying. We are called to get on all fours to let the mother and father in us out, then to let that sense of parenthood so permeate our being that we cannot help but serve those who are not as strong, not as bright, not as able bodied or able minded as we. Are we up to that task?

We're called to put our medicine bags under the noses of Pharmaceutical and Insurance Companies so that they loosen their unjust grip on health-care in America. We're called to advocate for anything that will help our 12 million children going to bed hungry every night in this most wealthy of lands, and to do something that will save the lives of 100's of millions of children dying each year of malnutrition and bad water. Might we consider advocating changes in the laws that have sentenced 2500 of the 2700 children world-wide to life-without-parole? Might we rattle the beads and shake our eagle feathers at Congress and our Governor to pass just and humane laws that disallow businesses to steal from the poor/helpless, while hiding behind the legality of fine-print contracts?

Christ was born into poverty so we can become rich in God's grace. Christ was brought into the world as a child, representing all the children of the world, so we might all stop talking, and start acting the part of good parents. After all, even Jesus called God: Father. Merry Christmas!

HOLY FAMILY: God, the family, wants that for us

I have been thinking about the Holy Family, and I've come to the conclusion that I am so lucky to belong to 2 holy families. I belong to the Samaniego clan and to the Society of Jesus, the Jesuits. Both are holy because both live the will of God for them.

God's will for a family has many facets. 1st, a couple must love and respect each other, open to help each other fulfill their personal dreams, that is, living up to the way they want to be remembered when they die. Then they must be open to have and raise their children as God's gifts to them and the world. That includes giving them good examples of being good persons, good marriages, and good Christians.

God's will for the Jesuits is to find God in all things and then to promote a faith that does justice. Using the Spiritual Exercises of St. Ignatius Loyola, we are to discern how God calls us and for what God calls us. Then God asks us to share that gift of discernment with those God sends us to serve.

My parents fulfilled their call to be good spouses, good Catholic Christians, and good parents of children, applying what was necessary according to each personality. They showed us how to love, forgive, serve, and to fight for what is right. How much more could God ask? They helped us to grow in wisdom and commitment, just like Mary and Joseph did with Jesus.

My province is fulfilling its call to be friends in the Lord in parishes, schools, and universities. Like good parents, our superiors give us the freedom to be ourselves, using the particular gifts God has given us to fulfill that call.

So, we celebrate today the call to be Holy Families for a world that tends to destroy families. We must challenge the institutions that divide families, such as I.C.E., governors that are elected to destroy immigrant families, working families, small mom-and-pop businesses, all of which erode the family structure.

We need to learn from Mary, Joseph and Jesus. They are a mixture of firm discipline and freedom that supports the individual's gifts. We must do the same with the people God sends us to serve.

If we want them to grow in commitment and wisdom, we need to be an example of these things to them. Wisdom and commitment are learned. Jesus learned them from Mary and

41

Joseph. We need to learn them and pass them on to our children. If our parents were not good examples of these values, we must learn them from other adult roll-models. If our children rebuff our wisdom and commitment that we have showed them, pray for them, and seek to help other parents and children to learn what's essential to be Jesus' disciples and apostles.

As we break bread this morning and as we recognize the presence of Jesus in the breaking of that bread, let us rejoice that we have so many people to learn from. Let us learn from the near-closing scene of Les Miserables. Let us take each other's hands and lead each other to salvation. Let us take each other's hearts for it is love that is everlasting. And let us remember the truth once spoken: to love another person is to see the face of God. May the world see that face in the way we love.

JAN. 1: MARY, MOTHER of GOD:
Mary's arms are open for us.

Over the centuries, devotion to Mary has grown in our Church. December is a month we celebrate the Immaculate Conception, the feast of Our Lady of Guadalupe, Christmas, and the Holy Family. In one way or another, Mary is central to all these feasts. And now we begin a new year with this feast: Mary, Mother of Jesus.

I believe that, since God to us Christians is three persons in one God, and since they are masculine: Father, Son, and Holy Spirit, then this feast is an attempt to show that God has all the qualities of male and female, of Father and Mother, and who best to show this than Mary.

Mary carried the mystery of the Incarnation, of God-becoming-human, in her womb and her heart. All mothers carry their children in their wombs, and later in their hearts. Since God has been identified with Love, then God carries all of us, God's children, in God's own heart.

Who but a mother is always ready to extend her arms to her children, no matter what they may have done or become? Who but a mother is ready to adopt an orphan and extend maternal love? Who but Mary could say yes to becoming pregnant outside marriage and confront the consequences, and say "yes" to looking upon the disciples whom Jesus loves and behold them like her sons or daughters?

Mary is a model of God's passion for us who are broken by hurts, mis-guidedness, misunderstandings, and we are broken by sin. Mary and Jesus have arms outstretched in mother-like fashion, determined to hold the disgusting, untouchable, abandoned, the motherless child in us.

Mary and Jesus want to save us from our darkness. Without their arms, their "yes" to us, we'd die in desperation. We are all here, full of hope for 2017, full of hope and joy, ¿for what? To better understand the mystery of Emmanuel, GOD-WITH-US. If we do this today and every day, then God will say to us, "blessed are we among women and men, and blessed is the fruit of our faith-womb: Jesus and his mission."

<u>EPIPHANY: God welcomes all outsiders!</u>

Every year we hear the wonderful story of Gaspar, Melchior, and Balthasar, the 3 magi following "yonder star" to pay homage to the new born king. Something about this story captivates most Christian people. What <u>is</u> their story? Perhaps, they're <u>outsiders, seekers, and latecomers</u>.

What are outsiders? Do they belong/fit in? No. Are they different? Yes! These 3 men are different, not from Israel. They were welcomed, made to feel at home by both Herod and the Holy Family. In Jesus' story the outsiders, the non-belongers, the Gentiles, were all welcomed.

Do we welcome the stranger, the different, the misfit, the outsider? Most of the time! How sad our nation no longer welcomes the different! We no longer live up to our Statue of Liberty's beckon: "Give me your suffering, your persecuted..." Governors are elected on anti-different slogans. Joseph & Mary welcomed outsiders. Are we like them?

The magi were seekers. "Where's the new-born King of the Jews?" They'd followed the star's light, met on the road and compared notes. They joined each other in search; they kept going, even with the possibility of not finding anything. Do you know people like that?

I've heard some say, "I feel like a hypocrite with my kids. I'm not sure I believe all the church teaches. I go to Mass yet my mind wanders and often I'm not into it. How can I believe in a God who allows babies to be born with AIDS, or when people condemn me for being gay or for being a woman feeling called to be a priest, or for being divorced? Why did my prayer not save my dad, child, spouse, job, or my health? Prayer is like talking to myself! I do it but I'm not sure. I'm a hypocrite."

No, they're seekers. Seekers struggle in faith. They are spiritually lifeless, but are faithful in their quiet, joyless, trip through life-in-the-dark hoping to see light, even if while not getting anything from it. Their fidelity, our fidelity, like the magi's was, will be rewarded with joy.

Lastly, the magi are "Latecomers." They arrived late. They dropped in out of no-where, looking odd, out of place; intellectuals in a simple place. It's unusual. Welcome to Jesus' story! They were wise men from the East, foreigners, Gentiles coming late to the banquet. We should feel at home with them because we live on Filipino time, Mexican time, and Vietnamese time; in other words, we, too aren't punctual. But, like the shepherds, they are accepted. They were the 1st "converts."

They bring strange gifts: Gold, signifying royalty; Frankincense, signifying holiness; and Myrrh, signifying the bitterness of death. Mary and Joseph would use these on their trip to Egypt to escape Herod.

All of us outsiders, seekers, latecomers, we are all welcome here. Do we recognize and welcome the outsider, the seeker, and latecomer in us? They are in each one of us and we are sacred in God's sight. That's the real message of the Christmas story. That's the real meaning of the Epiphany, of "God's Manifestation:" that we're loved as we are.

Our schools welcome outsiders. We value your children as gifts from God and we try and form them into boys and girls "for others." It means that we try to show them they're not alone and that others need the acceptance and love of God that can only be shown by them. As we celebrate Catholic School month, remember that school can serve as "God's manifestation," as epiphanies for your children.

This table makes manifest God's acceptance of the outsider, the seeker, and the latecomer in us. God accepts the gifts we are and those we bring, and God asks us to break bread as Jesus did for the outsider, the seeker and the late-coming disciples. May we recognize Jesus in the breaking of the bread, and may we let God's light come into the darkness of our doubts and fears. God welcomes us. Let us be grateful.

(Adapted from "Ever so Wise," Storytelling the Word, William J. Bausch, pg. 137-142)

BAPTISM of the LORD: Insights for Life!

There's a public school program that sends hired teachers to students that are in the hospital or incapacitated to keep up with their studies.

One day, a teacher received a call asking her to visit a particular boy. She took his name, the hospital and room#. His regular teacher said, "We're studying nouns and adverbs now. Please help him not fall behind." She didn't realize he was in the Burn Unit, and no one had prepared her for what she was about to discover on the other side of the door. She had to put on a sterile gown and cap to prevent infection. She was not to touch the boy or his bed. She could speak through a mask on her mouth. When she finished the preparations, she took a deep breath and walked into the room.

The young boy, horribly burned, was in great pain. She felt scared, not knowing what to say, but she'd gone too far to turn and walk out. She was able say, "I'm the special visiting hospital teacher, and your regular teacher sent me to help you with your nouns & adverbs." Later she thought it wasn't one of her better tutoring sessions.

On her 2nd visit, the Burn-unit nurse asked her, "What did you say to that boy?" Before she could finish apologizing, the nurse interrupted her, "You don't understand! We've been worried about him, but ever since your visit, He's a new person! He's fighting back and responding to treatment... it's as if he's decided to live."

The boy later explained he'd given up hope, feeling he was going to die, until he saw that special teacher. Everything changed with an insight he gained from the visit. With happy tears in his eyes, the boy, who had given up hope, explained: "They wouldn't send a special teacher to work on nouns and adverbs with a dying boy, now would they?

("Nouns & Adverbs," 4th Helping of Chicken Soup for the Soul, 1997, pg. 151-2)

On this Feast of the Baptism of Jesus, we ask ourselves, "If Jesus is God, why did he need to be baptized like we were?" I believe the boy's insight is the same insight that we need to see clearly: hope is alive in because God wouldn't send Jesus to help us work out our salvation if we were going to die, right? Jesus needed to discover his own life's mission: to show us God's love!

Many people feel life has burned them. They live in constant and hopeless pain, caused by life's burns and hurts. Many of us suffer and give up hope. That's why we need to hear a story like today's gospel, that God sent Jesus to show that He's one of us, and so honors our being that He'll subject himself to the same experiences, trials, and hurts.

Jesus, like us, is discerning his role, his reason for being here. He doesn't have it all figured out. He had followed his cousin John, listening to his mesmerizing words. He feels compelled to get into the water, to receive what the others have received. He received that and much more: a sense that God loves them, a sense that God cares.

As Jesus prays, heaven opens up an insight, one that impels him to go forth and live! "You are my beloved Son, in whom I am well pleased." The boy's insight was that a special teacher wouldn't have been sent to him to work on nouns & adverbs if he weren't going to live to use them. And our insight is: God so loved the world that God sent Jesus, a special teacher, to help us learn to live as sisters & brothers of each other & God.

What a gift God has given us! What a gift we are and can be for others if we but decide to do what we can do out of love. We began the Mass by placing our giftedness before the altar prior to asking to be forgiven. Then we prayed for that grace. Then we heard the 1st reading: God delights in our service, and in the 2nd reading: we're acceptable to God to preach the peace of Jesus. Then we gave each other peace.

Now we need to pray. Why? Because when the Church really prays, in one mind and Spirit, the heavens open up. Insights come when the heavens open up. Ours lead us to who we are, whose we are, and to whom we are placed here for. Let us be for each other, like the special teacher was for the boy: signs of hope in the care God has for us!

2nd in ORD. TIME: Share happiness and watch it double?

Tomorrow, Dr. Martin Luther King, Jr.'s holiday, we shall see President Obama inaugurated for a 2nd time. Today we heard read the theme of God's love for us much like that of a spouse for each other. Jesus and Martin both had dreams of a better world. Let us see Martin's:

"(We) must have a concern for self and feel a responsibility to discover our mission in life which shows concern for the welfare of others... Give priority to search for God. Allow God's Spirit to permeate your being... Make your plans (for life) big enough to include God and large enough to include eternity... Love yourself... That is the length of life. Love your neighbor as you do yourself... That's the breadth of life. "Love the Lord thy God with all your heart, all your soul, all your mind." This is the height of life...by painstakingly developing of all 3 of these dimensions can you expect to live a complete life." (Adapted from "Three Dimensions of a Complete Life," Best Black Sermons, 1972, pg. 7-17)

My 1st assignment to couples I prepare for marriage is to go and reflect on how they want to be remembered when they die. Did you know that Dr. King shared his ideas before his death? Listen:

"If you are around when I meet my day, I don't want a long funeral or eulogy ... Tell them not to mention I have a Nobel Peace Prize—It's not important. Tell them not to mention I have 3 or 400 other awards—It's not important. Tell them not to mention where I went to school. It's not important... Mention that Martin Luther King, Jr. tried to give his life serving others..., (that I) tried to love somebody... I tried to be right on the issue of war, ... I tried to feed the hungry... to clothe those who were naked... to visit those in prison. I want you to say I tried to love and serve humanity."
Ebenezer Baptist Church, Atlanta, Georgia, on 4 February 1968, by Martin Luther King Junior:

Mary loved and served her friends and told the steward, "Do what he says." Jesus loved his mother and told the stewards to fill the water jars. He'd do the rest. Jesus invites us to be filled with living water, and he'll do the rest. Do we believe this? Dr. King loved our country and so he described a dream about redemption and completion.

Out of concern for us, Martin saw what few in this country see: a nation able to hue hope from despair, transform discord into harmony, and doing it together. Isn't that hope-giving? Why would he risk his life to bring hope to the world? Someone once said:

There's tremendous happiness in making others happy, despite our own situations. Shared grief is half the sorrow, but happiness shared is doubled. To feel rich, count all the things you have that money can't buy. Origin unknown. Passed on to me from the Internet.

Paul teaches the Corinthians and us that we each receive the ability to manifest the gifts of the Spirit for some benefit, to make others happy. He shows us how to love the length and breadth of life. Mary shows us our need for height, too. By going to Jesus in faith, we show this height.

How do we measure up with these dimensions in our lives? Do our personal goals include God and others or not? Our schools both do! If our goals include God and others, our jars are filled with what Jesus can use. Do we have a relationship with ourselves and others but not God? This shows no height, and we'll burn out. Do we let others distract us from God? We're incomplete. We need to have our jars filled. This is where we do it: at the altar; at the wellspring of Catholics.

Mary showed Jesus that happiness shared doubles in size. Martin called the Preamble of the Declaration of Independence our nation's creed: "We hold these truths to be self-evident: that all are created equal, that we were endowed by our creator with certain inalienable rights to life, liberty and the pursuit of happiness." And Christ taught us all, including Martin, to live out our mission, which is God's dream for us. Martin learned quickly and gave his life in pursuit of it. How about us?

We've been given descriptions of visions that are possible for us all. Pray for the gift of love of self, others and God. Pray to see the benefit for the use of our gifts. If we do, we'll double God's happiness and our own.

3rd in ORD. TIME: Are you a moper or a hoper?

You know there are people who love change and joyfully look to the future for anything new. Then there are people who always look back imagining a time when things were seemingly better. Unfortunately, they also mope around in the present because it is not the past. They are not joyful, making those who live in the present miserable. Future people don't mind living in the moment, as long as there is a possibility of a better future. They bring people the joy of anticipation. Do we?

The author of *Habits of the Heart*, would say that the difference lies in having or not having a defined Mission. We heard Christ' today, and his disciples changed the world living it out. We recited ours as Mass began: "We discover God's love through worship, prayer, study and good works." Even, if we don't practice it fully yet, our school does. They recite it daily and discuss it regularly. They strive to live it out.

A true Catholic school or individual make a difference because they know whose they are and for whom we are here to serve and they serve only in love. A true Catholic isn't a moper but a hoper. A false Catholic mopes because they do not live as if they belong to Christ and for God's children. A true Catholic lives joyfully in the present, having learned from the past, and joyfully anticipates an even better future. A false Catholic lives out the adage that misery loves company.

To help us hope in a better future, let us look at a video of our school and listen to the testimony of some parents. We celebrate the end of Catholic School month by seeing how the future of our Church, our nation and our world are being educated.

Show the Video

Children learn from their parents, their teachers, their coaches and those they choose to be their mentors. Are they observing moping or hoping? The choice is always ours. Let us choose to teach them how to find hope in their lives, even when they're down.

4th in ORD. TIME: Are we part of Christ's function?

(This homily is a way of preaching to fund-raising. Every Diocese has a campaign to help meet the Diocesan needs. In San Jose it is called the Annual Diocesan Appeal, or ADA. This is an example of how to use your Mission Statement and relate donating or tithing to the Mission of the parish and that of the Diocese.)

Why is it that people put down the gifts and talents in another? All were amazed at Jesus' wisdom and words, and then comes, "Isn't he the son of Joseph…do we not know…?" In other words, "Isn't he just a simpleton?" Why couldn't they stay with the gift God had given them? Why can't we? Because we can't believe God can break into our world!

John Bradshaw is a counselor that has studied family systems. He says that in a dysfunctional family the peace that all families seek to have is focused on the dysfunction. For example, in an alcoholic family, all the members fall into their particular roles. As long as they live in these roles, there is peace. When someone decides to leave the role, chaos!

Bradshaw posits that the family can respond to that chaos in only 3 ways: 1st, they agree with the one who left one's role, and all decide to heal the dysfunctionality. 2nd, is the attempt to shame the "traitor" into returning to the role. The 3rd is ex-communication from the family.

Jesus embodies this theory. The scribes tried to shame Jesus into returning to the dysfunction of his people. When that didn't work, they eventually kill him, a permanent ex-communication. Today's passage is a precursor to what happened on the Cross.

Jesus tells the doubters that no prophet is accepted by his people. They respond with such anger that they wanted to excommunicate him. Jesus walks right through them and out of their lives. He realizes that he is called to leave home. Are we the people he was called to go to?

If we say yes, how do we show this? Do we respond with 1-1-1-1-1, or 1 hr. for each part of our Mission Statement? Jesus wants us to live it out. We want you to add an additional "1:" 1 hr. of your salary. Investing in the future of your parish says, "thank you to God and MHT."

That 5th "1" can help our diocese serve you. To help us understand this, we have invited a member of the seminary to share: (ADA talk)

<u>Seminarians came and presented their "ADA" talk here.</u>

5th in ORDINARY TIME: We're fishers for Christ

For those who loved Popeye cartoons as kids, remember his closing jingle each week: "I am what I am and that's all that I am. I'm Popeye the sailor man, toot-toot?" Our readings make us think: By God's grace, we are what we are; we are who we are. So, who are we? Whose are we? And, for whom are we here on this earth?

Our reading's characters shared <u>what</u> they were: sinners. Isaiah had an unclean mouth. Do we? Paul aided and abetted in the murders of Christians, his new brothers and sisters. And Peter said, "Get away from me for I am a sinful man" as a response to the miraculous catch. He was also the only disciple to be called "satan" by Christ. By being humble before God, he and the disciples received the gift of a vocation to serve.

We've been anointed to serve. To serve, we must admit to our dark sides, we must know our limitations and seek to overcome them. Do we speak ill of people? Do we overindulge food, tobacco or alcohol? Do we work too much or work-out too much? Do we listen too much to what others say about us, so that we have no idea who we really are? Are we whatever-aholics? Or do we just live in fear?

To overcome these limitations, we must come to know we're <u>not our own</u>. God so loved the idea of us, that God created us out of a loving heart. We are God's, and we are made in God's image and likeness. We were baptized with the <u>Holy Spirit</u> and with <u>Fire</u>. That fire is the fire of God's love, which is the only force in this world that truly heals. Do we believe this or not? What will it take to convince you?

Jesus says to Peter and us, "Don't be afraid, I will make you fishers of people." Can we trust that we, too, can cast our nets out into deep water and make a miraculous catch because Christ sends us? May we be humble and let God transform us! After all: "We are what we are and that's all that we are; we're Fishers, for Christ. Amen. Toot. Toot."

6th in ORDINARY TIME: Blessed are God's somebodies

A great Rabbi, noted for his compassion and service of his neighbor, received an unexpected visit from his 3 best students. It seems that they'd been arguing about why they were called to care for the poor and needy if they were considered being punished by God, and thus contaminated. They needed the Rabbi to settle the argument.

He took them into his study, opened the curtain revealing a huge picture-window. He asked each, "What do you see?" They each shared. "Good he said." He then opened up the door to his closet, revealing a body-length mirror. He asked them, "Now, what do you see." The 1st said laughing, "I only see myself." The others concurred.

The Rabbi asked, "What have you learned about your dilemma?" None answered. The Rabbi answered, "How interesting that a window and a mirror are made of the exact same material, glass. But the moment you line one side of it with silver, you cease seeing others & their needs, and only see yourself." The poor are not smitten by God. They are here to remind us to be grateful for all we have received and to show it in service of those who can't help themselves."

(Paraphrased: rewritten from: "Veneer of Silver," A Treasury of Jewish Folklore, Crown Publishers, NY, 1948, pg. 60)

The poor are not smitten by God. Yet are we grateful when we see those poorer than ourselves, for all we have received? Jesus fought against those who judged others by what they had or didn't have. He knew that when we confide in our things or wits, we are putting silver on the windows of our souls, our eyes, and we become egotists, selfish.

All our readings challenge us not to think or judge like society, building up lists of somebodies and nobodies. Society tells us not to trust our neighbor. But Jesus calls us to love our neighbor. Love is a type of trust, but without conditions. Are our hearts like trees planted near water, whose roots go forth to seek out Jesus, our living water?

St. Paul says that the only viable hope is that in Christ. In a way he presents us with a choice: Christ and Joy, or not Christ and a woeful life.

Our gospel juxtaposes Blessings and Woes. Blessed are the poor, the hungry, the thirsty, the weepy, and the persecuted for Jesus' sake. Woe to those who are filled in this life, for they have received their just reward. Because we know Christ, we reach out to the poor mentioned above. Doing so in Christ's name, we let our roots of faith go deep, and extend themselves toward the living water that Christ is.

Are we blessed or woeful? The choice is ours. Sometimes we find problems choosing among 2 goods. St. Ignatius, the founder of the Jesuits, knew this type of temptation. He said the closer we come to God and are blessed, the more the devil changes his temptation-tactics in order so we might choose the lesser of two goods.

For instance, am I called to be married or to be a religious. Both are wonderful vocations. Both are sacramental choices. But which is what God wants for me? Do we have the tools to make the choice? St. Ignatius would have us pretend like we already made a choice and live the rest of today and tomorrow as if I made one choice. At the end of the day, how do I feel? Do I feel at peace or not peaceful? Then live the next two days as if I made the other choice. Ask the same questions?

If we are honest with ourselves, if we really notice what our hearts feel like, we will know the answer rather quickly. One easy way to answer is to ask myself honestly, "Do I want to be remembered for having made the choice?" If yes, do it; if not, don't.

Jesus gives us choices each day. He gives us the opportunity to serve those who don't have what we have. Are we open to do this?

Let us recall that in this Sacrament God is calling us to have a be-attitude. If we do, we will be blessed. If not, we will hear, "Woe to you."

May we recognize Christ in the breaking of the bread, and see how blessed we are. Let us also give thanks for the people who are suffering and hurting right now for their faith, for theirs is the Kingdom of Heaven.

7th in ORDINARY TIME: The law of the echo

Those of us who have taken a bit of physics know that there is a law of physics that says, "For every action, there is an equal and opposite reaction." This means that what's put into an action, comes right back at you in the same amount. That sounds suspiciously like the words in the Gospel, "The measure with which you measure, shall be measured out to you." In other words it is the Law of an Echo. When you scream in a canyon, you hear your own voice bounce back to you. It echoes back.

Love, forgiveness, and compassion all follow the law of an echo, and so you can never lose by the Love you share, the forgiveness you give and ask for, and the compassion you show. They all return as blessings upon you. Today we are challenged to go the extra mile: "love your enemies, do good to those who harm you, pray for those who hurt you, lend without expecting anything in return."

How difficult it is to go that extra mile, but go we must. Why? Because, as one person once said, "Generosity is what marks a redeemed heart." If you know you are redeemed, you can't help but be generous. If you don't, generosity will never enter your mind. Alexander the Great was once asked why he threw gold coins to a beggar, when copper coins would have met his needs. He said, "Copper coins may suit the beggar's needs, but gold coins is what suits Alexander's giving."

Some time back in Florida, a crazy man took an automatic rifle and began shooting and killing people in a mall. By the time he was chased into a store, he had taken a woman hostage. You can imagine the desire for revenge in the town. The daughter of one of the women slain decided that she was not going to act on hate. "If I hate him, I am no more than a murderer...I have no choice but to forgive the man who murdered my mother." (Paraphrased from "Parables," Jamie Buckingham, Word Publishing, 1991, pg. 39)

Only a heart sown in Jesus' heart and his teachings can do that. Only those who are hurting, hurt other people. And only people who feel loved can truly love without conditions or borders. A grateful heart is a God-like heart.

Can we ask God for the grace to stop and think before reacting when someone harms us? Can we ask God to help us realize that when we hurt, we just might respond in kind to others? Can we ask God to imprint the law of an echo into our hearts so that we can recognize that good and evil both can bounce back at us when we act, so we always choose to do good?

There is a phrase that almost goes unnoticed in the Gospel: "Because (God) is kind to the ungrateful and wicked...Be merciful." That is what it takes to be called Sons and Daughters of the Most High. We are to be kind and merciful because God is kind and merciful with us. If someone hurts you, be kind. If someone slanders you, be kind. If someone makes fun of your faith, be kind. Kindness is of God.

Mercy is the ability to give freely to those who can't fend for themselves because we can. Mercy is the giving of kindness when all around you expect you to express your anger in an unkind manner. When we choose to be merciful, we choose to be like God.

Because of the grace of God, we must be instruments of God's grace for others. Can we be? The choice is ours. We can choose to love, to forgive, to show mercy and kindness and the equal and opposite reaction from God will be blessing. Lent is coming this week to help us to realize our capacity to love, forgive and be kind. Let us use this Lenten season to make the best choices, the ones that show we are God's.

8th in ORD. TIME: Is there a plank in my eye?

2 Buddhist monks out walking one day, came to the river's edge. The edge was all muddy from a storm. A beautiful woman, exhausted and distressed wanted across but couldn't make it. The older monk picked her up and put her on his shoulders and took her across, clean and dry. When they got to the other edge, he let her down. She thanked him and went on her way.

The younger monk kept walking with him for a few miles. When he could no longer take it, he stopped the older and asked, "I can't believe that you, a master, would let himself give in to temptation and let a woman touch him and let him carry her!" The older monk, with a kind, compassionate look, responded, "How is it that I left her off at the very moment we got to the river's edge and that you are still carrying her?"

(Adapted: "The Monk and the Woman," by Anthony de Mello,, Song of the Bird, 1981, pg. 108-9)

Boy, we like to criticize/judge another! Why do we forget what Sirach says: "the test of a person is one's conversation; a tree is judged on the quality of its fruit, similarly a person's words betray what one feels?" (Sir 27: 6-7) We forget to check whether we have a plank in our own eye <u>before</u> we try to take out the splinter in another's.

In John's Gospel we see a very similar idea: "By this shall all people know that you are my disciples by your love for one another." (Jn 13:35) How we approach another displays whether or not we love them. To really love another person one needs to understand human nature pretty well. We need to remember no one is perfect. We need to remember that we are all sinners. We need to remember that we are all <u>thous</u> in the eyes of God, and we are all called to treat another as a <u>thou</u> and not an <u>it</u>, like a thing.

That is why we 1st need to examine ourselves before we go to another with a problem we have with them. A Chinese proverb says: "When you see a good person, emulate them. When you see an evil person, take a good look at yourself." Why? Because we tend to show the most anger in another when we see the behavior

59

we most detest in ourselves. And since we love ourselves, and we do not want to lash out at ourselves, we find it convenient to lash out at another.

I know enough about myself to check out my feelings about a situation or a person before I confront the person. I know enough to examine my own motivations for pointing out a fault or an error or a habit, <u>before</u> I go to them with it. Why? Because I may be wrong, and because, even if I be right, I may have some prejudice or ill-feeling about the other that clouds the way I might confront them. Lord knows I have made mistakes and I don't want to repeat them.

I try to think about this: "What's the worst that can happen from the confrontation?" 1st, I examine the possible negative consequences. I bounce the situation off a person I can trust to be truthful with me. I share what the consequences might be. Once I have a clearer picture of this, I ask myself, "What's the best thing that happen from this confrontation?" If what might be lost is greater than what might be gained, or if more harm than good can come of it, I don't do it. I will not confront it right now.

However, if what is to be gained is greater, then I risk the rejection, I risk the initial anger or resentment in order to attain the good desired. This is the difficulty in what we call "the intervention." 12-steppers know that to "intervene" with an addict, with a compulsive whatever, one needs to have people that love the person, that have examined the situation thoroughly, that have clout or influence with that person, and that have a plan, a strategy in case the negative consequences occur.

The problem most people have is that they <u>react</u> instead of <u>respond</u>. Instead of examining the feelings, sensations, and after-thoughts that result from the negative encounter with a loved one, they just react. These always fall on deaf ears. These can cause great rifts in relationships. These are very difficult to heal.

I remember having a conversation with two friends of a friend of mine in the Jesuits. We were worried about his drinking problem. We examined the scenarios of the interventions we all wanted to make. This was nearly 15 years ago. We decided we'd go to him, one-on-one and confront him. If we had to do it over, we'd do it together.

When I took my friend out for a walk and shared with him what I saw in him when he drank, how his personality changed, how mean he got around others, how disagreeable he became, and that I felt he had a drinking problem, he exploded. For 4 years he refused to give me the sign of peace at Mass. For 4 years he refused to talk to or with me. I can't tell you how many times I pondered whether or not what we/ I had done was the right thing to do, because we seemed to have lost a relationship we had with him. Then one day, at the Ordination party, he came to me and asked me if I could walk with him. I said, "Sure!" My heart began beating rapidly, anticipating what was up.

He told me that he was in AA. He had gotten to the step when he had to make amends with those he had hurt, and told me that I and the other 2 Jesuits were the only ones who loved him enough to tell him the truth and that he had shut us out. He told me how sorry he was and asked my forgiveness. What a moment of love and reconciliation it was! 4 years of pain melted away in one instant. All was worth the salvation of a soul.

A tree is judged by its fruit. The conversation of a person is the test of that person. It may take years of pain, or a great rejection, or the total loss of a person's relationship in order to effect this change, but, if it is truly worth it, it must be done.

St. Ignatius says in his Spiritual Exercises: "We are created to praise, reverence and serve almighty God and, in so doing, save our souls. Everything else is created to help us attain that end." In order to save another's soul we must realize that our own salvation is linked with that. Last week's Gospel said, "forgive and you shall be forgiven... The measure you give is the measure you'll be given." Examine the measure of we're giving. Have we removed the plank in our own eyes?

If and when we do, remember that even the pain of loss is worth it if your heart is where your mouth is. May God bless us with that heart and bless the mouth that bears the Good News.

ASH WEDNESDAY: Have we died to self, or not?

Centuries of tradition shows us all that praying, fasting and alms-giving help us resist evil and gives us the discipline to change. If you listen to the Serenity Prayer: "Lord, grant me the serenity to accept the things I cannot change, the courage to change the things I can change, and the wisdom to know the difference," you know that it is a tool for discernment, for making good decisions. When we dare to live what the sign of the cross on our foreheads means, we show the world that we know the difference and that we are committed to change what we can change to bring us closer to God. But remember Matthew says:

"When you give alms...do not let your left hand know what the right is doing...When you pray, go to your room, close the door, and pray to the Father, who is there...When you fast, perfume your head."

We must pray like Jesus, who had a deep relationship with the Father. We must fast like Isaiah, who in chapter 58 says, "care for the poor, the lost, and the oppressed." And finally, give alms to our church and to the causes that serve the poor, for God hears the cries of the poor. Consider tithing 1 hour of your pay to the parish, which itself tithes each week to serve the needy, the poor, and the causes that serve them.

These are the tried-and-true practices that make the sign of the cross not just a sign. It says we want to be more like Christ. It says we accept the Way of the Cross. "Remember you are dust and to dust you shall return." Our life is what we do between the dust of creation and the dust of our burial. The ashes do not protect us from death. They are caused by death. They're signs of our death to our "self" and a "yes" to God, to follow Christ's example. It is the one day that separates us from all other Christian traditions. Let us wear the sign of the cross proudly for they tell the world "who" we are, "whose" we are, and "for whom" we were created to serve.

1st in LENT: What is our story of Lent?

Isak Dinesan once said, "to be a person is to have a story to tell." We have been spending time this week learning about journaling, and how it can be a form of praying, a form of telling God our story, and listening to God bless and encourage us to have the courage to continue the journey. Well, have you ever thought that the Bible is the journal of God's story as told by 72 story-tellers so we can know and love God?

Peg Neuhauser says that Storytelling is the most powerful way we communicate. In Storytelling we pass on the knowledge of our cultures, our families, and our history as a nation, a people, a church, everything experienced. It's how we entertain each other. It can destroy or build us up. It can encourage or demoralize. A good Storyteller can make us cry, laugh, think and even believe. And so we come once again to the story of Christ in the desert, tempted by the master tempter.

(Paraphrased from "Daddy, tell me a story," Dynamic Preaching, Vol. XXVI, 2010, pg. 57)

It's no accident that Jesus is the Word of God, for to know Jesus is to know God's Story. God knew that, to communicate with us, a story was the best medium. Today we get Luke's version of the temptation story. Like Matthew, the 1st temptation was to make stones into bread. Unlike Matthew, Luke puts Jesus on the mountain to offer him power over all the nations, then on the temple, asking him to test God and his angels to care for him. Jesus resists.

What can we learn from Jesus about how to resist our temptations? Well, we know that he spent 40 days in prayer and fasting. He left the river Jordan baptized, sent to learn about himself and his relationship to the Father, to resist his enemies, and to depend totally on God.

The devil tested his resolve and knowledge, just as he tempts us on our resolve and knowledge. He used food, power and the need for help to tempt Jesus. Why? Because all this was on Jesus' mind while alone with God.

Lent is the time for us to spend the next 40 days plus Sundays with God, who calls us to live our anointing and become God's storytellers. God calls us to accompany our catechumens and our

63

candidates in their journey with God. That journey includes prayer and fasting. Prayer is telling our story to God and God to us. Fasting is not just refraining from eating. Isaiah helps us understand what Jesus committed himself to do once he was to leave the desert. In Chapter 58 we'll find:

> "this is the type of fast I desire…release those bound unjustly,…set free the oppressed, … share your bread with the hungry, shelter the oppressed and the homeless, clothe the naked when you see them, and do not turn your back on your own." (6-7)

This was Christ's mission and it's part of our Mission Statement. Good Works, our 4th pillar, are what we used to call Corporal Works of Mercy. Praying is our 2nd pillar. So, has it sunk-in that Lent is not just 40 days, but a preparing and re-tooling for all the days of our lives? We are to be a Lenten People who put into practice Isaiah's fast, Jesus' prayer, and all in the telling the story of what God has done for us all as God's children.

So what can we do that we haven't already done? Let us look to do a noble thing every day this Lent. It doesn't have to be big, just noble. Be kind to each other and to anyone we meet. We can convert the world more with sugar than with vinegar. Look for the outcast and make them feel wanted and welcome. Look for the sad and tell them a story. Be alert for the moment our plans need to be dropped for a higher purpose.

Lent is not for giving up something, rather giving the best of who we are. Are we up to it? Then let us come to the table of recognition, where we will recognize our anointer in the breaking of the bread, and say "yes" to be the best storyteller of God's love for us that Christ has ever anointed.

2nd in LENT: Can you see it?

Fr. William Bausch shared about a day he was walking by a store's display window with some very interested college youths looking at it. As he neared, he heard them saying, "I see it!" with excitement or, "I can't see it yet," frustrated. He began to look at what they were looking at: a poster-size painting. It appeared to be a New-Age style. At 1st glance it seemed like a glob of painted strokes. More and more of the kids said, "I can see it now." He asked them what they saw, and they said, "Don't give up, keep looking, change your sight-angle, and it'll become clear." He looked, and went away frustrated to give a lecture. On the way back, he looked again and after a while, he saw it, and he exploded with excitement. In the globs of paint, the face of Jesus came clear along with three crosses in the background. He spent the next few minutes encouraging the others who had heard his "I can see it," to look and find for themselves.

(Adapted from: *60 more Seasonal Homilies*, pg. 52-53)

"Jesus took Peter, James and John up the mountain to pray. And while Jesus was praying, his face changed in appearance..." Can you imagine how they felt when, in the midst of their prayer, they could say, "I can see it now!" They'd been with Jesus so long and couldn't see it. "See what?" They saw who Jesus really is, and who it was who'd called them, shared time with them, and had brought them to God's mountain to pray and let their eyes be opened.

Have you ever looked back at your experiences and had your eyes opened to a truth you hadn't noticed before? I spent my sabbatical time doing just that, and I can say that, looking at my life, taking time to look over my past, that I, too, had my eyes opened to the reality of God. That opening of our eyes is our own Transfiguration experience.

Why is the Transfiguration so important? All 4 Gospels note the effect it had on Peter, James and John, so much so, that it transformed them into the leaders of our church in the 1st Century. That means that our Transfigurations will change us into bold tellers of God's story. We too are called to be Fishers of people.

To fish, we need the right tackle, rod, reel or net, and the patience to spend hours fishing and telling stories, while God does the work behind the scenes.

We are made in the image of God. Jesus was made into the image of us so that he could help us see in the painting of God's world, God's face. We are blind to God's face in our own lives because we spend not enough time looking, reflecting, and changing our angles of vision so that we discover the face of God in the painting of our lives. It is like the movie, Dead Poet Society, when Robin Williams jumps atop of a desk to let his students see that we sometimes have to see the world from other positions in order to see the reality of the path our lives are to take.

Jesus offered that to the three apostles. Jesus offers that to you and me by inviting us to pray this lent. Prayer is spending time looking at God and God's art-work so that our eyes can see, and our hearts become opened only to the joy that that vision can bring. Take the time to look over your past life and see it from the angle of the present and in the light of the future. Don't give up. God's face is there. See it and let that "Aha experience" transfigure your life before the eyes of your friends, family and church. Then we can say together as Peter, James and John said, "It is good for us to be here."

3rd in LENT: Be patient! God ain't done with me yet!

*For parishes with RCIA candidates/catechumens, we use the Year A readings for the next 3 weeks. However, here is a homily for the 3rd Week that uses the actual readings for the day. They can be adapted to fit the theme of baptism for our catechumens.

"Have faith, our vine dresser will give us a 2nd chance!" Let me take you on an imaginative journey of words.

"Well, do you know what a great God we have? I'm Jesse and I work this land together with my wife Vita and my 3 daughters. We've planted every tree and vine you see for miles. I know everything about these plants. I'm proud of them and I love them.

The master knows little about them except what I tell him. I know every tree will bear fruit. Some take more talking to, others more fretting over, and still others are more challenging. Each demands a different approach in order to get them to become joyful and bear fruit.

They remind me of my daughters and what it's taken to raise them. We began treating each the same. That didn't work. We had to spend a lot of time with each one, to get to know what each needed from us as parents. Then we responded to those needs, letting each know that we loved them, in both action and word.

Trees, like my girls, are jealous. Each perceives that the other is more loved by us growers or parents. Each needs to be convinced that the love we have for each is equal, but different. That's the most challenging lesson of all to get across. Why? Each hears, feels, and responds differently to stimuli. Each tries to be who they aren't. For example, that fig tree told me it had heard that the best tree to be is an olive tree, due to the value of its extra virgin oil in making great food. It concluded that figs aren't wanted.

Imagine how hard it has been for me to convince the fig tree that that is what it is called to be. The reason it has taken so long to bear fruit is that it still doesn't believe this. People are very much like this. They spend long periods of their lives trying to be who they aren't when all God wants is for them to be who they are.

Trees, vines, and people are not so different. Each is lovable, each is sacred, and each is gift. To find this out takes time, and, it takes making mistakes. Getting them to see that each is gift is the task of a good vine dresser or good parent. A good one never gives up on one's plant or child.

So, imagine what I felt, when the Master said to me, "Chop down that fig tree!" I screamed inside, "No!" But what came out of me was, "Give me another chance, I'll do something new. If then it gives no fruit, I'll chop it down." What the Master doesn't know is that I will never cut it down.

Fig trees take time to bear fruit. If it gives no fruit this year, I will convince the Master to give me another year, and another. I love that tree, and I'll never give up trying. I, like Moses, have discovered that this ground, this tree, these children are holy.

We are holy. God willed it so. We're holy ground. You are called like I was: 1ˢᵗ to bear fruit that will last, and then to take your turn at being a vine dresser in the Master's vineyard. Once you have learned to be a good vine, a good fig tree, then you will be called to tend to your own vine or trees as if they were God's own. Do we love our vines enough to never give up? We have a chance and a choice to make. Let us be the best disciples, that is, learners we can be, so that we can leave Mass as apostles, as vine-keepers, that tend the vines and trees with love and help them bear fruit.

If you believe this, step up to this holy table and celebrate with me. If you don't quite believe this about yourself, then step up and leave your fears, doubts, and desires at the foot of this table, and remember, Christ, our vine dresser, always gives us another chance. Step up and ask for the fruit of His love for us: His life. Take and eat, take and drink for this is holy food. And do this in memory of Jesus.

4th in LENT: Brothers will be brothers (sisters, too)!

We've come here in Lent, experiencing and working on our inner-life to prepare for Easter. We look at our dreams, and like our Biblical ancestors, we experience God's voice and presence as God's way of being with us. Let us look at the Prodigal Son story with new, Lenten eyes!

We've been challenged to accept and love ourselves just as we are, not unlike the 2 sons in the story. Like the younger son, we feel like our older one, the always-obedient goody-2-shoes, but never knowing dad's praise. We learned to resent our older brother due to the perceived preferential attention received from our dad. Like the older son, we feel unattended to by our task-master father, who spent inordinate resources on that ingrate of a younger brother.

In both cases, the father made mistakes. In both, the sons did, too. We feel a bit nervous because we don't have much experience in what to do about the rifts. So we look at how we come to reconciliation, and how it deserves to be celebrated. Is reconciliation simply forgiveness? No! Reconciliation includes forgiveness, but it's much more than that. It's the renewal of communion with each other.

When children play, they sometimes hurt each other. They express their anger, sadness, or pain, sometimes with tears, other times in rage. But, how long does the rift stay a rift? Not long! Why? Because, children value more the relationship than what caused the rift! If they hold onto the rift, they'll stop playing. And so they learn to reconcile.

The separation in the parable pains both the son and father. Both take time to reflect upon what happened. The son recognizes the love of his father in the midst of his pain, hunger and shame. Dad recognizes his faults and vows to make amends should the son return.

Awareness of what both did to cause the rift had to happen in order for healing to occur. It took both admitting to themselves they'd been wrong. It took both coming half-way, giving in a little, in order to be truly reconciled. It became a win-win situation. That's why the father called for the grand celebration: he got a 2nd chance to show his love and mercy towards his independent, yet foolish, son.

So, what about the older brother? He, too, insulted his dad like his younger brother had done, by refusing to enter the party given by his father. This would have been embarrassing to him, because the older son's place was by his father's side. The story has no resolution.

We're left to ponder what we would do. The father realizes he made a mistake with the older son and meets him more than half-way. If the older had recanted and gone in, not only would by-gones have been by-gones, but the party would have escalated. The father would have saved face, and the older brother would have taken his proper place as son and heir. That didn't happen, however; or at least we don't know.

How many of us have difficulty forgiving? How many of us can let go of past hurts, valuing more the relationship than losing face? How many of us are prone to jealousy and envy?

If we're prone to these, then we're more like the older brother than we care to admit. If prone to these, we won't believe God does not count our transgressions against us and calls us to be reconcilers, shalomers in God's name.

Can we see hope in the Prodigal Son parable? Can we examine our consciences and move on with life? Then let's celebrate here at the table of communion. Always feel here the invitation to renew our communion with God, who meets us more than half-way. Let's be reconciled so we can enter into deeper communion with God on retreat.

5th in LENT: It takes two, doesn't it?

How many of us have had negative things happen to us and feel that there is nothing positive in our life? Well, the 1st reading says God will provide water in the desert. In other words, some positive thing will happen in the midst of apparent negativity. Most people think of the desert as a barren, forsaken place. Yet God tells us we're chosen, formed for God's self. In other words, we're a present for God made by God. So, in the midst of our distress, God sees the positive and tells us.

What keeps us from finding the positive? How about fear, pain, depression, persecution, trauma, and injustice? Death, illness, prejudice, torture, abuse, betrayal, and abandonment also do their part of keeping us down and feeling negative. We just lost our brother, Gerard. It's hard to see the positive in our feelings or experiences, but they are there. We are better for having known him. However, most negative feelings make us remember moments in our past.

We replay them, letting our feelings of fear, anger, revenge, or rage paint new scenarios for these old experiences. The longer we live in the past, the stronger the negative feelings build up. These are the most destructive feelings we can face. Yet face them we must.

The best way to face them is by learning to say, "From now on." Jesus said these 3 words to the woman caught in adultery. Once he'd written on the ground and the condemners left, he said, "From now on, avoid this sin." He forgot her past and gave her back her present and hope for the future. In other words he is saying: "From now on, choose life." What is past is past, live only in the present.

The word, Present, is a word with 2 meanings. Present is something we give and something we live. We give a present, and we live the present, meaning now, in the moment. To live in the now we must forget both the past and future.

We, who live in the now, know we've received a present: the gift of life. This truth sets us free. Do we trust it? Do we let people drag us down by reminding us of our past? The past should only be learned from, not lived in. Those, who live in the past or long to return to it, fear living and stop living. Jesus wants us and the woman to remember what's been done for us, not what we did. We must remember "From now on...," forgetting our past to return to living only the present.

"Do this in memory of me" has new meaning for us now. We gather to hear and to do what Jesus says: "From now on, love one another as I have loved you; forgive each other as I've forgiven you; heal each other as I've healed you; listen to each other as I've listened to you; and, from now on, challenge each other as I challenged you." Doing this strips us of our past, clothes us in the present, and so transforms for the future.

It's not too late. Our past accuses & condemns us. Christ challenges and invites us to live "From now on." Can we learn from our past by finding the positive in the negative, and live it now? Can we see that Jesus really has placed *rivers of living waters for us on our way through our own created deserts?*

Come, let us celebrate at the altar of invitation and transformation. Let's give thanks to God for not counting our sins against us. Let's give thanks for Christ's gift of 3 words: "From now on..." Let's prepare for Holy week by getting on our knees a little more this retreat-week and write in the dirt of our lives the very sins that Christ forgot and forgave. Let us do this in memory of Him. We will not be disappointed.

<u>PALM SUNDAY: We have an unusual Pope.</u>

We celebrate how normal people felt excited that one of their own was entering into his glory. Instead of entering Jerusalem like Pilate did: on a big, white horse, Jesus entered mounted on a simple ass. The same animal that brought Jesus into Bethlehem, that took Jesus to and from Egypt, brings him into the City of Peace: Jerusalem.

All types of people were there to see the event. With whom do you identify most? Do you see Jesus as one of you? Do you see Jesus as a star you are observing? Do you feel proud like the disciples must have? Or do you feel afraid for him as those closest to him must have felt? I imagine the Swiss Guard is feeling that way around Pope Francis.

Pope Francis caused a huge stir by announcing he is not celebrating Holy Thursday Mass at St. Peter's or St. John Lateran. He has chosen a juvenile detention facility. He is visiting the imprisoned as Isaiah and Matthew compel us to do. He is setting the tone of his papacy in order to give us an example as Jesus will at the Last Supper. His 1st homily challenged us to save the earth and serve the poor.

He humbly asked us all to pray for him, and so we shall. He is leading the way in a manner not usual in a Pope. Can we follow his example? Our Mission Statement carries a 4th pillar: Good Works. Can we commit to doing Good Works in the coming year? If so we will have chosen the road less travelled by, and it will make all the difference in the world. May the holiness of Jesus and Pope Francis rub off on us all.

HOLY THURSDAY:
Discomfort is the 1st step to letting God in!

Can you imagine sitting at a special dinner and the host, taking a towel and a tub filled with water, kneels down and asks you to remove your shoes and stockings or shoes? How would you feel? Odd and uncomfortable, no? Well, now we know how Peter and the rest must have felt. Peter just happened to say what everybody else felt, "You shall not wash my feet!"

Jesus, however, uses the awkward moment as a teachable one. He tells Peter and the others that one-ness with him involves service, the lowest service reserved for a slave in his day. He wants them to know what God expects from apostles. Jesus tells them that he is showing them an example for their future as apostles, as those "sent" to do like he did. Peter, as usual gets it, but goes a bit overboard with his response: "Then wash my head and all over."

Well, tonight the Lord hands us the towel of servitude and says, "You know what you are meant to do. Wash." But the act of handing us the towel is a reminder to do what we have been trained to do. So, we have a choice: either we humble ourselves in order to serve, or we let our pride get to us and reject the call.

The commandment we hear tonight is a recalling of what we are called to do, anointed to do: to serve others. And tonight we hear that Jesus, our teacher and master calls us to follow his model for he has shown us time and time again what it takes to "have a part" with him. Do we want to be a part of our Lord, or not?

"Love one another as I have loved you," he says to every one of us. Indeed, he says it in such a powerful way: he gets down on his knees and washes the feet of his disciples. We need to get over letting others serve us, otherwise we won't know what to do or say when we turn around and expect them to let us serve them.

So, get over it and start loving as we have been loved. Then we can sit at God's table and break bread with the God who loves us till the end.

GOOD FRIDAY: Can we find peace in Christ's suffering?

We just heard: "We do not have a chief priest that doesn't know our weaknesses, but one who has been challenged in every way we have." This should console us, because there is nothing that Jesus has experienced that we haven't experienced.

Who has never felt abandoned, betrayed, hurt, or made fun of? Who has not felt the loss of a loved one, whether family or pet? Who hasn't been falsely accused of something? We have all been through all these, and Jesus, too!

Nevertheless, Jesus didn't react like we would have. He, having taken the cup his Abba gave him, said, "Not my will but thine be done," leaving all negative feelings and accepted what was to come with peace.

I had a conversation with a husband who just lost his wife of 22 years. Boy did he love her! He was angry and agitated with God for being unjust. He exhibited frustration, desperation and rage. When he finished his story, he said, "I am leaving my faith. I no longer believe in God, for the God of justice will no longer be in my beliefs."

I asked him, "Before you wife died, was she peaceful or agitated?" "Peaceful." "And was she someone of great faith or was she an unbeliever?" "She had a great faith." "Well then, why don't you return to the scene immediately before she died, and see if there is any connection between her faith and her peace?"

When I said this, I watched his face change. He no longer felt anger toward God. He felt that his wife had said many things to prepare him for her death, but he was not ready to accept. He realized that she had tried to console and strengthen him, but he had not paid any attention. I told him, "It's never too late to return to the scene and let yourself be healed."

That is what Jesus says to all of us who are agitated with our life's situation. He says, "I know how you feel. I have felt as you have. Learn from me. If I took the cup that my Father gave me, why not take mine? You will feel the peace it brings." That is the message of Good Friday. "Come to me all of you who are weary and heavy-burdened, and I will give you rest."

Let us rest this day and tomorrow in the Lord. Let us return to the scenes of Jesus' passion and our experience of loss or death.

Let us be healed by then. That way we can celebrate with joy at the Easter Vigil the resurrection of Jesus, our savior. We can feel the peace that only God can give.

EASTER VIGIL: Do we witness to the existence of God?

Rabbi Abraham Joshua Heschel once wrote: "There are no proofs of the existence of God: there are only witnesses."
(Adapted from an excerpt of: "He is alive!" Dynamic Preaching, April 1993, pg. 3)

When pushed by people to show them God exists, we can only fall back on our experience of how God has worked in our lives. Nothing can ever convince a person of God's existence more than a bold teller of the inner truth we carry. Mary Magdalene was pushed to tell her story, one that was rejected by Peter and the rest. "Crazy woman!"

They needed physical, visible truth to be convinced. But Jesus said to them all, "Blessed are those that have not seen and still believe." That word "those" refers to you and me. We are here because we saw, and we believe. We've seen God's presence in ourselves, in our brothers and sisters, and in our magnificent world and universe.

A famous writer once said that there are 3 distinctive markings in the life of a true Christian: a Tranquil Mind; an Unquenchable Joy, and an Outgoing Love. When we pray as if everything depends upon us and work as if everything depends upon God, we have peace of mind. Tranquility comes when we know we are God's instrument in the symphony of life.

A priest was a guest in a 2nd grade classroom. He asked the kids what Jesus said when he rose from the dead. One kid raised her hand with excitement. When called, she said, "Tah Dah." The joy of a child can capture us if we see everlasting life as ever-laughing life. Joy's infectious, let's catch it.

When we fall in love with a person, don't you want the world to know? We can't help but want to shout it out. For God so loved the world, he forgave it for it knows not what it does. For God so loved the world, that he knelt down and washed the feet of the very ones who would betray, deny and abandon him: us. For Christ so loved the world, that he took the cup of God's plan for him, and drank it down and then refilled it so that we too might drink. For God so loved us that he sent us those who are to be baptized, confirmed and receive the bread of life and the cup of our salvation and mission.

When we take and eat tonight, when we take and drink tonight, let us do it together with a tranquil mind, an unquenchable joy, and a love that only knows one direction: out. Let us trade our tomb of sadness and depression and trade it in on a womb of gladness and enjoyment. Let us rejoice and be glad for God-with-us has kept his promise. Let him rise in us tonight and for the rest of our lives.

EASTER SUNDAY: Are we born-again?

A man was born twice from the same woman. One day he was driving his mother to a funeral. She'd been to many--her husband's, her brother's, and most of her friends'. She was out-surviving those she knew, but not without pain and grief. She'd lost her money, had a heart-attack and bouts of uncontrollable crying and depression. Hers was a troubled old age. As they drove along, she calmly talked about her wake and funeral.

She had instructions to impart and wanted them carried out. Suddenly she said, "I'm giving up on fear!" Her son looked over and their eyes locked. This was the deepest they'd ever conversed. "Everybody dies! Nothing is left. I'm giving up on fear." She said it as a matter-of-fact tone of voice. For to her it was no big deal.

"I've tried it," her son said, "It's not that easy." He'd been haunted by fears all of his life: fear of sickness and death, of the future, of losing his money or his job. In one moment of insight it dawned on him he'd lived his life in fear. Fear had so structured his life, he felt almost imprisoned by it; it was the main motivator all of his life.

Looking at his mom, he noticed her face beaming. They never talked about it again, but his mom began to change. She'd never been shy about sharing an opinion or two, but now she spoke her mind on every topic, without pomp or self-righteousness, but with an authority, no, a wisdom from her heart, laden with understanding and a tolerance of the human condition, and it was full of gentleness and strength.

People wanted to be around her. They could not say what she gave them, but they knew they were richer for encountering her. It took more than 9 months this time, but she gave birth to his spirit. It had been huddled deep amongst the dark and frightened parts of his soul. It needed some careful combinations of breathing and pushing, but it came forward. Years ago, she had given birth to his body, now she gave birth to his spirit.

Jesus knows this and understands. Once a woman said to him, "Blessed the womb that bore you and the breasts that nursed you! He answered: "Blessed the one who hears God's word and keeps it." He said it not to correct her, but to state a parallel truth. Mary gave birth to Jesus. But it took the interaction, the relating day by day with him that gave birth to his Spirit. She and Joseph raised his consciousness above fear to the higher reaches of love. He, too, was born twice.

(Adapted: "The Spirit is a 2nd Womb," in Gospel Light by John Shea, pg. 94-96)

This rebirth is a gift. We're here because we were once reborn of water and the Spirit through a woman: Holy Mother Church. She's not perfect, nor has she ever been. But errors do not destroy the Spirit, as we saw in the young man and in his mother. Errors or mistakes can lead one to depression, negativity and fear, but they can be overcome. It took mom saying, "I'm giving up on fear," and acting it out to do it. She changed forever. It changed the son. It changed Jesus, too, for he had been fearful.

When we came to Sangre de Cristo, some of us were tired from many years at the same place. Some of us were wounded by superiors or the work itself. We came with doubts of faith, depressed about life. But we came with hope that the experience would recharge, reform, and rebuild our sense of faith and hope for this love-starved world.

I'm sure we are different now than when we came. God and Sangre has made it so. We've looked at fear in the face and decided to give up on it. We will use the following weeks to continue the process of leaving fear behind in this nurturing environment made possible by the Christian Brothers of LaSalle and their collaborators. We will leave here having been born again for a third time.

We see the cross as a symbol of fear and symbol of victory. We are freer now to choose how it will be symbolized in our lives. If we believe in the leaven that faith-filled people who love us and nurture us have given us, then we can be living bread for each other. What do you say? Can we continue, once and for all, and leave our fears at the foot of the cross? Can we live the rest of our lives as men and women changed by God's grace? If so, then let us celebrate our being reborn in God's Spirit. Let us break bread and recognize Jesus, who calls us to do likewise in his memory. Let us celebrate our own re-birthday today.

2nd in EASTER: Even Jesus doubted.

Who here has not had doubts at one time or another? We've all come here to Most Holy Trinity from all over the world. From listening to you, I've heard doubts of one sort or another: some are serious and some are more normal. What's great here is that we can all identify with the fact that we are people of faith and people of doubts, and that is OK! Even Jesus doubted; even a future saint like Mother Theresa did!

It seemed to shock people when it was found out in her diary that she had doubts. Was she doing the right work for her? Did God really exist, and if so, did God really care? How can someone who has doubts like these be considered for sainthood? "Father, take this cup away from me, but not my will but thine be done!" That was Jesus doubting. Well, these examples should console us, along Thomas in today's Gospel, too.

Jesus, Thomas, and Mother Theresa are examples for us. Doubt is an invitation to stay faithful. They did. Thomas' reaction to the others' excitement is very normal for us who've grown up with the "need to see, hear, or touch" generation. Mother Theresa's reaction to a world out of balance is normal as well. Heck, how could Christ not doubt in the moment of his impending death? Yet, they didn't let doubt get the best of them. Remaining faithful, they received confirmation of their faith.

Do we all react the same way when life deals us pain, when a loved one dies, or when we lose a job, or when we don't get the job we really wanted? No, we don't. Some of us need the company of our loved ones in order to cope with pain or loss. Some of us need to be alone to think, reflect and to decide what's next. Some of us are talkers and need to share everything. Others of us are listeners, getting to our own solutions by listening to how others are coping. Some of us are born leaders, capable of helping direct and inform the wills of others. Others of us look for that strength in others. And still others need to do it all alone.

Jesus, Thomas and Mother Theresa needed to cope by themselves before coming to check it out with the others. Thomas, depressed at having lost Jesus, wanted to be alone to think. Once he did, he came back to the group where he was hit with a surprise.

Whatever the reason, he reacted needing physical proof. I'm reminded of a story:

> Many people like to say: "I don't have to go to church. I can worship God in my own way." Well, someone said that to an old, wise priest on a winter's day by a campfire. He got up and took out a glowing piece of coal and put it on the stone hearth. As both watched, in a very short time the coal went out. He asked, "Did you notice? Faith is like that coal. To maintain itself it needed the fellowship of other coals, and we of others."
>
> (From "Who is Thomas' Twin?" in <u>Telling Compelling Stories</u>, by William J. Bausch, pg. 112)

We, like that coal, need others to have the fire of faith be rekindled and burning brightly. To keep the fire burning we must add new coals to that fellowship. That is what our Neophytes are: New coals. Thomas and Mother Theresa needed coals, too. Thomas took it to the extreme of not believing until he could see and touch. Isn't he a bit like you and me? Mother Theresa saw and touched God's Kingdom's least and believed.

We are here because we have all bought into the mission of Jesus, to recall and rejoice at having placed our fingers and hands into the wounds in Christ's body in the world. We are here to have Christ himself remove all doubts that we have made differences in the world. We have formed a community of faith-filled burning coals, and that has steadily removed most of our doubts.

We have huddled together, acknowledged the pains and wounds of our past, in order to see, touch and believe like Jesus, Thomas, and Mother Theresa. When we break the bread of our faith-lives, let us say "Amen" to the mission of our next assignments. Let us do so saying like Thomas, "My Lord and my God."

3rd in EASTER: Get hooked and go fishing!

There are two types of people: those who like surprises and those who don't. Peter loved surprises, Thomas didn't. Thomas was not happy when the others told him they'd seen the Lord. Peter, on the other hand was overjoyed when the disciple whom Jesus loved said, "It is the Lord." It didn't take Thomas long to come to believe, but he had to see and to touch the Lord. Peter was so excited, he put on his clothes to jump in the water to see him.

This excitement is what we saw on Holy Saturday night when we baptized 39 new Catholics. We see it when we baptize new infants, too. We're excited to have left one form of life and embrace a new life. The beauty of seeing adults baptized is seeing the apex of a process of growth from hearing beliefs, to living a faith. Living a faith is not easy. Why?

"Faith is not taught, it is caught!" If so, then are we caught or just fishing? Well, I must say "yes" to both questions. I hit a crossroads in my life in which, although being a cradle Catholic, I chose this faith, this Church, and what it means to be Catholic. My faith became my own.

I now love attending Mass and being a part of a community of faith and its practices, which I felt blessed by doing, and others felt blessed by seeing me do it. So why "yes" to both? Aren't they either-or questions? No. They are both-and questions. Though I chose to be Catholic, I realize I need others, a support group let's say, to strengthen my faith and to connect with others so I don't feel alone in this walk. When I connect with others like me, we allow Christ to flow through our unity.

In realizing the need for others, I cope with adversity in whatever way it raises its head. Tests and trials can challenge faith, create doubt, or sneak in when our defenses are down. That's when we most need to go fishing. That is why Peter and the boys had to go fishing: to think about what to do next.

By being open to God in our lives, God can come in. It's that openness that helps me get hooked over and over again.

By spending time in the presence of God and being aware of it, I can see both fishing and being caught as opportunities to be with God. It is an incredible journey, this faith walk of ours. Get on with your fishing and let yourself be hooked.
Paraphrased from: "Are you still fishing?" by Ian Mascarenas

There's no better fishing hook than knowing we're loved. That's why Jesus said, "Love one another as I have loved you." He knew that he had hooked them with his love. He wants his disciples to hook each other by loving each other. Love is what feeds faith. That is why Paul said, "The greatest of these (faith, hope and love) is love." Only love can come to say: "Father, forgive them for they know not what they do."

That "them" includes us! Are we fishing or are we getting hooked? If we're in the fishing mode, let us do it together, as a community of fishers. Fishing alone is like golfing alone. If you catch a big one or hit a hole in one, who can you share it with? Let us be caught and fish together. We will have God's joy, and have it to the full.

Only someone who's hooked can answer "Do you love me?" with "Yes, Lord, you know everything, you know I love you." Only someone who goes fishing can be ready to jump in the waters when one gets hooked. Either way, like Peter, we need a community.

So, let's go fishing today, and let ourselves get hooked by the God whose very life is alluring to us all because of God's love for us. Let us approach the altar of God's fishing love-boat as a community, and let ourselves be fed like the apostles were on that beach. Once we bite into God's lure, let ourselves be sent to go fishing for others who don't know what they're missing. And, most of all, let us go into a world of wayward fish, with the same net that the apostles dragged on that shore. We will be blessed with quite a catch.

4th in EASTER: God's love knows no bounds!

In belonging to a group, belonging has certain responsibilities. Today, when so few people own up to their responsibilities for their actions, we need to look at sheep for good examples of action. What does being a good sheep require of us? Well, the gospel tells us that "my sheep hear my voice and know me." In this day and age of noise, are we able to discern the voice of God? God's good sheep know the voice and heed it. It should console us that God knows our voice as well.

There's a tribe in Cameroon called the Hdi. A translator found out that all their verbs ended in the vowels: i, a, or u. The use of the vowel determined its meaning. Now interestingly enough, their two words for love are dvi or dva. They never use love as dvu. The translator tried to find out the significance of the ending for love. He asked, "Could you dvi your wife?" They said, "Yes, meaning that the wife had been loved but now the love is no longer there." "Could you dva your wife?" The answer was "yes" as long as she remained faithful and cared for her husband. He through them for a loop by then asking, "Could you dvu your wife." All present laughed saying, "Heavens no! If you did that, you would have to love her no matter what she did, even if she got you no water, or made you meals. Love as dvu doesn't exist."

The translator asked, "Can God dvu the people?" The Hdi leaders pondered the question, they began to cry. "This would mean God would keep loving us over and over, millennia after millennia, all the while we rejected his love. God would be compelled to love us, even though we've sinned more than any of people." After the discussion, the 3rd word for love, dvu, was added to the translation of the bible, to depict the type of love God has for us, without conditions.

(paraphrased from: "Belonging to Christ's flock," Dynamic Preaching, April, May, June, pg. 14-15)

The Hdi people discovered what the Greeks knew all along: that there are 3 words for love. God's love of us is dvu, a love without conditions. Would we weep if we honestly believe we are loved without boundary or conditions? I pray that we would, for that is God's love!

God loves us more than we know, and God calls us, sinners all, but with the ability and gift to choose to live or to die, to help the world live in God or die outside of God. So, are we attuned to the voice of God in nature, in others and in ourselves, or not? If yes, then we have the gift of discernment, the ability to distinguish among the many voices vying for our attention, the voice of God. That gift will help us stay on the path.

To receive that grace, we need to spend time with God, we need to pray. If we love God above all else, we should want to spend time with God. Do we? Do our lives show that we are following Jesus? Do they show that we love our neighbor as God loves us?

Christ is both the Lamb of God and the Good Shepherd. The Good Shepherd knows the voices of his sheep. And his sheep are not just Catholics or Christians. He said he has other sheep not of this fold, and he is their shepherd, too. Now, if Christ has 2 roles to play in life, that of lamb and shepherd, and he is our model for loving God, neighbor, ourselves and the universe, don't you think that we too have 2 roles to play in life? We, as sheep, are to recognize and respond to the voice of our Good Shepherd. We, as shepherds, are to recognize the voice of God amidst the voices of the sheep entrusted to our care.

Both roles have their place and time in our lives. We must know what it is like being lambs so as to know what to do to make listening with discerning ears the call to the sheep entrusted to our care. God speaks always and in all ways, but it is we who tend not to listen. Listening is not hearing. Listening is hearing with an intention.

Let us pray today thanking God and Mother Earth, for giving us the wheat and grapes we will share in the form of bread and wine. Let us thank Jesus, whose mission becomes our own when we respond to his call. And let us thank God for making us the sheep that, when belonging to God's flock, can become food that feeds and tends the lambs we are entrusted to care for as Peter was called last week.

5th in EASTER: Change or die!

Fr. Adolfo Nicolás, S.J., the General of the Jesuits wrote in a letter to us all that we must change or die. He implied that we must keep up with a changing world and influence it. There is a problem, however: most humans resist change. Why? Some resist because they fear it! Some resist because they are too comfortable to leave their "zone!"

We Jesuits are trained to be ready to move at any moment and not to become too attached to anything other than promoting a faith that does justice. Hence, if Fr. Adolfo said what he said, he must be seeing the Society not as available as trained to be.

For me, a Jesuit and a pastor, I always want to leave a place better than I found it. After being here 10 years, I believe our shared vision together has changed MHT, and for the better. Jesus tells his disciples: "By this shall all (people) know that you are my disciples: by your love for one another." (Jn 13:35) Nothing changes a person more than knowing they are loved. I believe we have love for each other. Sometimes we who are too close to the action can't tell, but new arrivals to MHT see it.

An 87-year old student in my philosophy class came up and said, "I'm Rose. I'm 87. Can I give you a hug?" I laughed saying, "Sure, go ahead!" She gave me a giant squeeze. "Why college at such a young, innocent age?" She jokingly replied, "I'm here to meet a rich man, marry, have a couple of kids, retire and travel." "Seriously?" I asked. "I always dreamt of having a college education and now I'm getting one!" she said.

After class we walked to the student union and shared a milkshake. We became instant friends. For the next 3 months I was hypnotized listening to this "time machine" as her wisdom and experience soaked me. In just a year, Rose became a campus icon making friends wherever she went. She reveled in the attention bestowed upon her from the other students. She was living it up. At the end of the semester we invited Rose to speak at our football banquet. I'll never forget what she taught us. She stepped up to the podium, and as she began to deliver her prepared speech, she dropped her 3x5 cards. Embarrassed and frustrated she simply said, "I'm sorry. I gave up beer for

Lent and this whiskey's killing me! I'll never fix the cards, so I'll just tell you what I know."

As we laughed she cleared her throat and began, "We do not stop playing because we grow old; we grow old because we stop playing. There are only 4 secrets to staying young, being happy, and achieving success.

"Laugh every day. Have a dream! Lose your dreams and you die. So many walk around dead and don't know it! There's a huge difference between growing older and growing up. If you're 19 years old, lie in bed for a year and do nothing, you'll turn 20. If I'm 87 and do nothing for a year, I'll turn 88. Anyone can grow older. It doesn't take any talent. To grow up, always find opportunity in change.

And finally, have no regrets. The elderly rarely have regrets for what we did, but rather for what we didn't do. The only ones who fear death are those with regrets." She concluded by singing "The Rose." She challenged us to study the lyrics. At the year's end Rose received the college degree she always wanted. A week after graduating, she peacefully died in her sleep. Over 2000 students attended her funeral in tribute to the wonderful woman who taught by example that it's never too late to be all you can be. The following words sum up Rose's loving memory:

REMEMBER: growing older happens, growing up is chosen.

Read between her lines and you'll see Rose's love for humanity and for being human. Her advice is as true now as in her time. We don't stop playing because we grow old, we grow old because we stop playing. We need to laugh every day, especially at ourselves. We need to identify and live our dream, the dream God put in our hearts: the one in which we make a difference that we've lived at all. We need to grow up by seeing the opportunity that change affords, stop blaming others for our bad choices, and get on with life, with no regrets.

You've seen changes and will see more. You'll soon have a new pastor. I'll have a new job. We all face a choice: embrace change or fight it. Rose embraced it even at 87, and made a difference in over the 2000 who mourned her. We need to embrace the changes that are inevitable.

If we trust that God is in the change, it will lead us to feeling consoled. "Behold, I will make all things new." That "all" includes MHT, you, and me! We're called to grow up with no regrets. Embracing the changes God sends is the way to no regrets. Fighting change will lead to regrets. Choose wisely.

6th in EASTER: Remember!

A person once said that the purpose in life is to make memories. Writing them down is a wonderful way of being able to take them out in the future, when our bodies start to deteriorate and we can no longer work as we once did. When I came here nearly 10 years ago, I had just closed my memory box of my previous parish, Christ the King, in San Diego. I came here with a new box, hoping to add memories that I can share with whomever wants to hear them.

My vision for parish work in general, and for MHT in particular, has not changed. I sought to build a community of communities that prays together, struggles together, plays together, dreams together, cries together, and implements together. I want a parish that is child, youth, and young-adult-friendly.

I cut out a comic strip from years ago. It shows the priest greeting people as they leave the church. A little child looks back as if to the altar and says, "Thanks God. I had a great time today!" I dream of a parish and a Church that is that joyful and that grateful all the time.

In 10 years we've grown into the model parish that we are together. Together we have learned about the theology of seeing. Seeing has to do with the eyes above our nose and those we call our inner eyes. Without the gifts of sight and insight, how can we say we know and love God?

A professor of Cosmology shared a phrase about the gift of sight and insight: "We must learn to see God in all things and to see all things in God." Her passion for that phrase reminded me of the Jesuit notion of being "contemplatives in action," which means finding God's presence in all things and responding to it with loving compassion. Do we discover God's love as our Mission Statement says: through Worship, Prayer, Study and Good Works? Are we contemplatives in action?

Christ said, "Whoever loves me you will keep my word." Simply put, we are to love God with our whole self, and love our neighbor as we've been loved. I am sure that the apostles did not know what all that meant, and so Jesus also promised the Holy Spirit who would teach and show them everything. God created the whole universe in an explosion of love. Since God is in everything, we are to love everything as God would have us love it. That's why Jesus said, "Be my witnesses to…the ends of the earth." We must witness to God's love of us.

So how might we love all that God has made? We start by caring for ourselves. What we feed our bodies, minds and spirits show that we care or not. What we do with our water and the land shows if we care for the globe we call earth. Are we reaching out to the "have-nots" of this world as our new Pope Francis has asked? It seems that the bottom-line is our new God. Hoarding things instead of good relationships seems to be the way of the USA.

If we are to hoard anything, let us hoard memories. Life is too short to spend our time more with things than with the earth and each other. We must give God the gifts of our gratitude for and love of all that we are and have received. "By this shall all know that you are my disciples, but the love you have for each other."

As long as 10 years are, they have flown by quickly. Is your memory box of MHT as full as mine is? It is not too late. All we need to fill it is to see God in all things at MHT, and to see all things of MHT in God. Then we can say as the song says, "I once was blind but now I see!"

ASCENSION SUNDAY:
How do we handle our "in-between-times?"

2 angels tell the disciples: "Why do you stand here looking up at the skies?" Don't you just love those who try to make things better when you don't want to feel better? They don't realize we need *in-between-times*, transitions, in order to heal, to get our lives in order, and move forward.

Hence, we've come to the Church's *In-Between-Time*. It's between the time between Jesus leaves his friends and disciples behind, and the time the Holy Spirit, the promised Consoler, comes. Jesus leaves them to ponder the future, to deal with his absence, and to move forward in life. The Holy Spirit is coming to help them do all this.

I don't know about you, but this made me think about my own *in-between-times*. Did any images or ideas come to your mind? How many of you went away to college? How did you feel when you walked out the door, or when your parents, who helped you move in, left you? (Pause) You see? You've had an *in-between-time* in your life.

How many of you moved from your neighborhood during your childhood? How did it feel to leave all the familiar surroundings, the familiar neighbors, plants, trees, animals, smells, colors, friends? (pause) Again, you've had an *in-between-time*.

How many of you have lost a family member, a friend, or a pet to death? How did you feel the moment you found out? What about the time right after finding out? (Pause) This, too, is an *in-between-time*. This is the type of *in-between-time* the disciples had once Jesus left for good.

The disciples stay looking at the sky, wondering where Jesus had gone, pondering what he'd promised them while alive, and trying to deal with it to keep going. The angels were right in questioning them. They were right about their having to get on with life after Jesus. They were right to remind them that Jesus would come again. They were being forced to deal with the facts in the in-between time and move on.

If we don't deal with our *in-between-times* and with the feelings they bring us and our family/friends, we can't understand what was happening to these friends of Jesus. Not only that, but we can't really help loved ones and friends deal with their *in-between-*

times. We'll only be able to say: "Do as I say and not as I did," the kind of statement that helps no one.

How did the disciples deal with their in-between time? The Gospel says they fell down to do him reverence, they prayed. The combination of prayer and the angel's words left them filled with joy. Later they'd be found constantly in the temple witnessing to the mighty deeds of God.

So, we're given a way to deal with our *in-between-times.* We must pray admitting our need for Jesus to heal the hurts, the emptiness, the homesickness, and to let Jesus infuse us with the joy and peace that only he can give. And finally we must share with anyone who'd hear just what God has done for us, in other words evangelize.

Pray, let go and let God, and evangelize: 3 steps to making our *in-between-times* opportunities for growth and grace. Can we pray for what we need today? Can we let God shape us and form us? Are we willing to share with each other what God has done for us? If so, let us be grateful, for this is a grace of the Consoler, the Holy Spirit. If not yet, let us pray at this table for the grace to let God use us. May God bless our teens and others going through tough *In-Between-Times.* And may we be like the angels, telling those who just look, to stop looking & get on with sharing.

PENTECOST: The Holy Spirit is God's Post-it!

Satis Prasad, a Hindu priest, was interviewed by Norman Cousins. Satis had come to the USA to be a missionary. Norman thought he had come to convert our citizens to Hinduism. He was wrong. Satis had come to convert us to Christianity, because, to him, Christianity had become a custom, not a way of life. So he came to convert us and our leaders to put to practice, what we preach.

(Paraphrased from "You might be a redneck if...", Dynamic Preaching, Vol. XVIII, No. 2, 1998, pg.54)

What a statement: "Christianity had become a custom, not a way of life." Satis understood that for most of us who claim to be Christian, our actions and decisions show we're far from Christ. Today we celebrate Pentecost, the birthday of the church, when God came intimately to us.

John's Gospel says: "The Holy Spirit...will teach you everything AND remind you of all that I told you." This has made me think that the Spirit is really God's Post-It. What's a Post-it? It's a clever invention: a paper with a sticky strip on the back. You write a note on the front and stick it on the wall so you can't help but see it, a reminder of what to do.

Satis and the Holy Spirit remind us that words are cheap and what is needed is Action. Our actions speak louder than our words. St. Francis of Assisi said it best: "In all things preach the Gospel and, if necessary, use words." Do our actions let people know we belong to Jesus Christ? If arrested for being Christian, would they have evidence to convict us?

Do you remember how boastful the disciples were prior to the Judas' betrayal and Peter's denials? They bragged about standing with Jesus, even in death. Well, we know what they did. But even when Jesus appeared to them after the Resurrection, they were afraid. So Jesus had them wait together in Jerusalem, for the coming of the Holy Spirit.

Once the Spirit came, "All of them were filled with (Her) and began to speak in other languages, as the Spirit gave them ability..." They were imbued with many gifts we call charisms, and became part of "the rest of the Story." Once the Spirit gets a toe-hold into our souls and hearts, it is we who can't let go! Once exposed to the Lord, Jesus can do things in and with us we can't begin to imagine. That action we celebrate today.

There are 3 ways to know that the Spirit is present, in control: 1st, a transformed life; 2nd, no walls between believers; 3rd, an empowered Church. If we're the same now as before our baptism and confirmation, then we're blocking the Holy Spirit's work. If we claim Christ as our personal Lord and have not forgiven our neighbor or served the poor, then the Spirit isn't at home in us. If God's people are not empowering the Church to make a difference, then we are Spirit-less.

To know our gifts the Spirit has given us, answer this: how do we want to be remembered when we die? Are we living that way right now? If yes, we've been empowered to do what God inscribed in our heart. If not, then we're not working with the Holy Spirit to transform the world.

To be personally transformed we must live as if transformed. If we do not help others become more joyfully engaged in Jesus' mission, then we are not serving as God's post-its for action. It's the Holy Spirit's power to influence that must flow through us. The Spirit is freely given. We must freely accept her.

"How much is a pen worth? It depends on who's using it. How much is a sprinkler-head worth? On a shelf, nothing, but if attached to a water-line, it brings much life. And how much is a human worth? Apart from God, very little! But connected to a loving heart and a visible faith, a human can be a powerful source of hope, a post-it for Christ' Mission.

Catholic Charities serves as God's post-it in San Jose. Listen, so we can respond generously to their pitch.

TRINITY: Good deeds are the way to God!

What a statement in Proverbs: "I take delight in the human race." God's love for us is quite big, no? Listen to a story of discovery:

In the film, "The man who played God" a great, famous & rich musician began to lose his hearing, and it depressed him. He grew angry at the world, abandoned his friends, family, and even God. He moved away and began to learn to read lips. From his window he'd look out onto the park with his binoculars. He practiced reading the lips of the people speaking in the park.

One day he concentrated on a kid whose lips were moving in prayer. He figured out what the kid was asking God for, and sent his servant to give it to him. Later he read the lips of a lady telling a friend what she needed and had to have. Again the musician sent out his servant to give it to her.

Each time he did a good deed, he'd look up to heaven and laugh at God. He thought to himself, "How funny it is to play God when I don't even believe in God." He kept on doing good, and something in him changed.

The man who played God found himself with God. Through the game of satisfying the needs of others, the real God in whom he did not believe made God's-self real to him. He discovered God is the God of relationship, one that serves the rest. *(Paraphrased from: "The man who played God," World Stories, William Bausch, pg. 283-4)*

Do you ever wonder why we so stress our Mission Statement? We discover God's love by doing. Our "doing" is worship, prayer, study and Good Works. Another word for good works is "good deeds." We stress doing good works because in so doing them, we become more and more like God, who delights in us. Our God so loves us that God doesn't let us leave for long. Christ revealed a God that is relational. The man in the story discovered this by fulfilling the needs of others.

The man in the story grew angry at God and the world because he was losing something, his hearing. Who of us hasn't grown angry at God for something we lost? I have often heard people get angry at God for losing a spouse or other loved one. I have heard anger in the voice of those who lost a job, a house, a pet. Anger is a sign of relationship. And you know, it's ok to be angry at God. God can take it. In spite of our losing our way to God, God relates with us, because God is family.

Father, Son, and Spirit, they are one and they are three, and there is no way to explain it except by analogy or metaphor. If you take three keys on a piano separately, you hear three distinct notes. If you play a particular three and play them all at once, we hear only one sound, and we call it a chord. One chord made as a combination of three notes. Three candles have separate flames when lit. Join them together and you have only one flame, and the three others are indistinguishable from each other. Thus is God. Three persons separately, but are one God, who delights in seeing us relating as they do.

The only time God is sad, is when we stop relating as they relate. You see, we are made in God's image and likeness. We are most like God when we relate as God does, and God relates only in love. We're most human and divine when and only when we love each other. If God would ask: "How's your love life," How would you answer?

I've had 9 months to ponder that question, ever since I told you that my time with you was drawing to a close. This is our 10th and final Holy Trinity together. We have shared a lot of love over the years, and we are called to continue sharing that love with each other and with all who come and grace this holy place.

I hope that we all commit ourselves to lives of service, lives of good works, even when we don't completely believe in God. Why? Because God, our mysterious Holy Trinity, is greater than our beliefs! God is greater than our defects, greater than our sins, greater than our ways of judging and condemning.

God delights in the human race. We must remember this, even when we have lost our way, or even if we stop believing, all we need to do is a good deed, filling the need of others, and somehow, some way, we will be changed into the image of three in one love.

Eduardo A. Samaniego, S.J.

CORPUS CHRISTI: Let's loaf around!

We celebrate Corpus Christi, the Solemnity of the Body and
Blood of Christ. These should be symbols of unity and peace.
Look around you. You are to be symbols of unity and peace as
well. We are of many cultures, languages and customs, and we are
many, but we are one because we will partake of the same loaf.

You, who know me, know I love to play with words. The
word loaf can mean 2 things: as a noun: a loaf of bread, and as
a verb: "to loaf" means to laze around. We eat one, and live the
other. We eat to live with the loaf of blessed bread, & we live to eat
by sharing our loaf with others.

So let us examine the connection of one loaf with faith.
Most of you simply believe communion is something you receive,
someone you get, something that becomes a part of us. A few of
you really get that the one loaf we eat is so that we become what
we eat. We don't just get the body and blood of Christ; we are to
become the body and blood of Christ. When we leave here today,
we are to feed a love-starved world. If we don't we become loafs
of the faith, in the worst sense of the word, loaf.

We listened to Luke's Gospel. Jesus challenged the apostles as
he does us, "feed them yourselves." To understand what it means,
we must go to John Ch. 4. Jesus tells his apostles that his food is to
do the will of the one who sent him and to complete his work. So
to eat Christ's body and blood is to take in his mission. We're sent
to complete his work, which is to preach to all nations the truth
of God's love for us all. We don't get communion, we become
communion.

To be important in the world one must have things: money,
fame, and status. To be important to God, we must give of ourselves,
we must serve the rest. It is the Good Works pillar of our Mission
Statement, mirroring Christ's own mission. To be number one in
God's eyes one must become servant of the rest in love.

Service tends to tire one. That's why we need food for the
journey of service. Our communion bread and cup are food
enough to convert us into instruments of God. For 52 years MHT
has done this, and we've done this well. We feed each other in
many ways.

I've often told you <u>faith</u> is not a noun but a verb. Well, it's the same with Communion. Communion is a commitment to go out to the world and fulfill Christ's mission. It's not about <u>me</u> and Jesus. It's about <u>we</u> and Jesus. Communion with the Body and Blood of Christ reminds us that when one part of a body suffers, the whole body, mind and spirit suffer. If Jesus isn't our source of unity and peace, of our compassionate service and justice, then the whole Body of Christ suffers. Paul's letter to the Corinthians says this.

So, let us give thanks today for 52 years of living our faith, hope, and love, for the wisdom life brings, for the gift of discernment that identifies what's of God and what isn't, and for the gifts of healing and reconciling. Let us give thanks for being able to see God's presence in all things, including ourselves, and seeing all things in God. By uniting in this act of Thanksgiving, this Eucharist, we are one body in Christ. When we act with compassion and love, we are the Blood of Christ outpoured.

So, what do you say? Are you ready to give thanks? While we're at it, let us give thanks to God for our new Pope Francis, our Bishop McGrath, our former pastors, associate pastors, and our deacons, who have served over these past years.

We have a legacy of hospitality, of great liturgy, of great preaching, and of Good Works of mercy and justice to live up to. May we celebrate our 52nd birthday as the body of Most Holy Trinity with joy and peace.

Let us eat the Loaf, be the Loaf, and share the Loaf of God's love and compassion with a world that is desperately hungry for it.

11th in ORD. TIME: Good fathers, like God, love fervently!

"One to whom little is forgiven, loves little." Did you know all Jesuits make the 30-day Spiritual Exercises of St. Ignatius? The grace of the 1st week is our heart learns we're loved sinners, called by God to praise, reverence, and serve the God we love above all else. We learn we've been forgiven much, leading us to love God expressed in a greater love of neighbor.

Like Simon in the Gospel, too many of us today have no idea we're sinners. Like Simon and his fellow Pharisees, we feel self-righteous, and so we judge others harshly. This leads to a tepid love of God, and an even more tepid love of neighbor. Simon fixated on <u>what</u> the woman was, and not on <u>who</u> she was. "There will be more rejoicing in heaven over one repentant sinner than one righteous person not in need of forgiveness."

Christ saw repentance and rewarded it with forgiveness. Her need for God, her loving faith, saved her. Simon's lack of love, led to his forgiveness not even being mentioned. In fact, Simon and friends, fathers all, were put down for their lack of hospitality, their lack of a discerning eye, and their lack of lifting burdens from the backs of sinners. God, our Father, through Jesus, forgives our many sins. We need to let this seep into our hearts so that we love not tepidly, not lukewarmly, but fervently.

Good fathers love fervently. Good fathers teach their children how to love, how to forgive, and thus, how to be happy. I was blessed to have a father who did this for me and my 8 brothers and sisters. My father loved life and loved humanity so much that he'd wake us each day whistling *Réville* and saying: "Time to get up; it's a great day for the race!" We'd all answer with, "What race dad?" "<u>The human race!</u>" That is how he began his day and ours.

As a priest, I've seen all sorts of dads, and I can't help but compare them with my dad. In fact, I compare all dads, even God, with my dad. But I must say a real dad has a huge cross to bear, but for real dads, it's no problem carrying it. Real dads communicate with their kids, sacrifice themselves for them, and will do anything for them. Why? Because they love their children!

There's no greater gift a dad can give his children than gratefully acknowledging God's gift of life and God's gift of faith that responds to God and neighbor in loving acts of service. We celebrate that today. Our Mission Statement is an expression of this fact:

<u>We discover God's love through Worship, Prayer, Study and Good Works</u>.

The 1st step to this discovery is what we celebrate at the beginning of the Mass: the Penitential Rite, and what we celebrate when we pray the Lord's Prayer. If we take the rite and prayer seriously, we make God rejoice at our repentance for having failed to love as we are loved. We leave our gifts in the back or in our pockets, so that we can reconcile 1st with our neighbors, our brothers and sisters, for we all call God, Abba, Father! Remember this when we make our offerings after the prayers of the faithful! Remember this when we hold out our hands and say, <u>amen</u>, at communion!

Discover God's love, be grateful for it, and show that gratitude in an attitude of loving service, loving Good Works. Let us do this and we will one day hear God's word say: "Go, your faith has saved you!"

12th in ORD. TIME: Paul was rad. Are we?

Did it ever occur to you, kids, that St. Paul was a "Rad" kind of guy? Did you ever think that one of our greatest saints sometimes opened his mouth before realizing what he'd said? How many times have you been accused of doing that? If it makes you feel better, St. Paul did this, too.

I believe this passage from Galatians is the most radical statement in the New Testament: "Neither Jew nor Gentile, neither slave nor free, neither woman nor man in Christ." If that is not bold, what is? To get the meaning of the statement we must understand why Jesus asks: "Who do you say that I am?" You can't understand one without the other, and we must answer it one day if we are to become true disciples of Jesus.

We've seen all politicians say things, whether they mean it or not, in order to get votes. St. Paul said many things, in order to get true converts committed to Christ. St. Peter boldly said: "You are the Christ, the Son of the living God," and won Christ over. But once you've said things, you can't take them back.

Politicians are held accountable for what they say. St. Paul was held accountable, but fought for and won one of the 3 statements he so boldly made: <u>Neither Jew nor Gentile</u>. It took 1800+ years for the 2nd of his statements to come true: <u>Neither slave nor free</u>. Many of us today are asking if it'll take 1800 more to make the 3rd of the radical statements come true: <u>Neither woman nor man in Christ</u>. As *radical* as it is, pursue it we must.

But to pursue something we hold dear, we risk being rejected or being told that what we hold doesn't matter. Jesus risked both things when he asked his disciples: "Who do people say that I am?" And, "Who do <u>you</u> say that I am?" Jesus asked to find out if his presence had made a difference, and if his message was getting across. He risked finding out if all he'd done and said meant that he had failed.

It's like when you can't wait to see what your report card looks like, or when you look at the cut-list of people who made the team, the band, the play, or the club. Your heart pounds with anticipation. A part of us can't look for fear of finding out we had failed. Jesus was like us. Once he knew he hadn't, he became bold again, just like when we bragged to others we had made it, and that we <u>never really</u> were nervous, right?

That boldness can lead to us say things without thinking. St. Paul realized later how radical his statement in Galatians was. He changed his verse later not to include "Neither woman or man in Christ." The trouble is he said it and he can't take it back.

Now <u>we're</u> the ones who have to account for the reality and truth of his statements. Now <u>we're</u> the ones to whom Jesus asks: "Who do you say that I am?" Who is Jesus? He's God. He's the one who heals us and makes us feel like somebodies when society makes us feel like nobodies. He's the one who comforts, feeds and calls us <u>just as we are</u>, to complete his mission. To recognize <u>that</u>, is to deny ourselves and carry our cross and follow Jesus. Only when we're able to answer: Who are You? and Who is Jesus? will we be able to say that we are disciples of the Lord.

What say you kids? Are you ready to fight for the completion of the most radical statement of the New Testament? If yes, I must warn you as Jesus warned his disciples: you "will suffer many things, and be rejected by the elders and the chief priests and the scribes." Just as in Jesus' day, they will put you down.

To complete Jesus' mission is to risk being chastised and rejected. But to do so with the Lord at our side is to "Lose our life for Christ's sake, and save it." May we all be saved by the God, who weeps bitterly as a mother weeps for her first born because of His great love for us!

13th in ORD. TIME: We are called

When we're baptized and confirmed, when we say, <u>amen</u>, to receiving communion, we promise to follow Jesus and complete his work, his mission. We make the promise freely, but are we promise-keepers or promise-breakers? We commit ourselves to follow, yet we will leave here today as apostles, sent by me as followers <u>and</u> doers of Christ's Word.

One of my favorite songs is "We are called." Its lyrics say, "We are called to act with justice, we are called to love tenderly, we are called to love one another, to walk humbly with God." It's taken from music written for the Easter Vigil, as baptism music, while the newly baptized are getting dressed.

The song expresses what's behind our readings today. To respond to the call and to being sent with a mission is to be fit for the kingdom of God. It means we must leave here ready to set the hand to the plough that prepares the soil for the seeds of God's Word. If we leave not ready to do so, then we are proving we are not fit for God.

Do we experience God's love so much that we want to sing about it? Do we experience it enough to follow so that we always feel it? Do we experience the call to act justly and respond, to love tenderly and share, and to walk humbly and so follow?

Today's Gospel says: "When the days drew near for His being taken up, Jesus set his face to go to Jerusalem." Something had to trigger that response. Jesus had a purpose and made a choice: to be homeless and show his total dependence on God. He chose to confront those powerful enough to put him to death to show us the depth of his love for us all.

Most of us have trouble making good choices, because we live in fear and trembling, or work hard to control the uncontrollable. How do we overcome these feelings? Ask, "How do we want to be remembered?" The answer points us to our true calling. Next, <u>act</u>! We must act justly, that is to do the right thing in all times. And finally, be grateful for the knowledge and courage to act upon that knowledge.

Are we ready to make a difference in this world? Then I invite you to sing along with me:

"We are called to act with Justice, we are called to love tenderly, we are called to love one another, to walk humbly with God."

14th in ORD. TIME: Peace begets peace.

There is an adage I first heard in Spanish: "It's the temptation that makes the thief." Listen to a story about the power of the living God.

A would-be-thief noticed a car that was left unlocked in a typical mall. As he approached the car from the rear, he also noticed a bumper sticker that read: "Peace be to you." The thief got in the car and then left a note on the front seat. It said: "Dear owner, I fully intended to steal your car until I noticed your "Peace be to you" sticker. It really made me pause and think. If I stole your car, you would not be at peace, and I would not be at peace either, since this was to be my "1st job." So peace be to you as well as to me. Drive carefully, and next time, lock your car." Signed: A Would Be Thief.

When you hear the word peace, What images, feelings or emotions are conjured up for you? Comfort? At ease? At-home-ness? Security? Sleep? All is well? I can be myself? Well Being? Right relationship? Joy? Happiness? Freedom? Powerful words, no? All these can apply to Jesus, am I right? So peace stirs up a few images for you and for me.

Did you know "peace" in the Bible can mean 4 different things? 1st, a military peace is the peace between warring nations/ peoples. 2nd, is a personal, well-being kind of peace: to be at peace with ourselves. 3rd, is the peace of being in right relationship with God. And 4th, Peace is used to imagine a global peace with God, where all creation rightly gives God praise. Do we give God praise when we share the sign of peace?

It's for peace that we're baptized. We were washed in water made holy by the Holy Spirit, who alone can bring peace. And for this mission we have been called. "Blessed are the peacemakers, for you shall be called children of God." In Hebrew the word for Peace is "Shalom." So we have been called to be "Shalomers" for Christ.

How can we help bring peace to the world? We can feed the hungry and clothe the naked or the needy like our pantry does. We can visit and comfort the sick as many of you do. But there are many and more difficult ways of bringing the peace that only Christ can bring.

What about the families that put up with abuse of any kind, be it physical, mental, sexual, or drug abuse? Sometimes peace comes only by setting limits with consequences that might mean separation from the homophobic or physical abuser. That type of peace-making is tough love. It brings peace to the household that shudders in fear and can be held hostage by the addicted member or the abuser. It can also bring peace to the abuser if he/she reflects, as the would-be-thief did, and then takes the necessary steps to heal oneself.

What about those who work for World Peace trying to abolish the presence of weapons of mass-destruction, or to eliminate the wanton destruction of the rain forests and other resources God has given us God's children? What about those who return to the battlegrounds of our city streets in order to help eliminate the violence between hoods, races, genders, sexual preferences, between ages past and present, between political ideologies? They are shalomers for those with eyes.

How difficult it is to sow the seeds of the Peace that only God can bring. All of these are what our families are encountering each day, sometimes alone because they don't want the neighbors to know. To them I say, "Peace be to you!" To them we are sent 2 by 2 in order that we might be true "Shalomers" of the Risen Lord in support of each other.

Let us renew our "Yes" to God to be sent so that we might have peace, which brings the joy made complete by Jesus. Let us give each other more than signs of peace today. Let us truly BE peaceful.

15th in ORD. TIME: A Samaritan for the ages

What a Gospel! If Jesus were to test us as he did the scholar, how would we fare? "What must I do to inherit everlasting life?" "What do the Scriptures say?" "Love God with your whole heart, your whole strength, and your whole mind, and your neighbor as yourself." "Who of them was neighbor to the one left for dead? Who showed compassion?" "Go and do likewise." What's compelling to me is that the Jews of Jesus' day did not believe in everlasting life. They did not believe in the after-life. So this scholar had to be from a reform movement.

We have two scenarios: one a dialogue between Jesus, who knows, and a scholar who claims to know. The other is the story that holds up a dreaded Samaritan as an example of being neighborly to those who hated the Samaritans. That is like holding up Clinton to a republican as the example of citizenship, or holding up a Catholic to a Pentecostal Christian as an example of discipleship. It would be that shocking.

Do we limit or hold back our love? Of course we do, because only God loves unconditionally. The priest in the Gospel moved on because he obeyed the book of Numbers (19:11), which says: If you touch the body of a dead person, is you are ritually unclean for 7 days. The priest would miss his turn to make the offering. Limits.

The Levite knew that the road to Jerusalem was dangerous. To walk it alone is to be foolish. The beat-up man was foolish, and the Levite walked on, dressed as a Levite, like a priest in a Roman collar in Skid Row. He was afraid to stop. Understandable, but we see limits.

The Priest and the Levite were being good and wise citizens in the eyes of the disciples. Then Jesus shocks them with the Samaritan, and so our idea of good citizenship is not God's idea. You see, no limits. As for me, I love the inn-keeper. What a trusting soul. Imagine someone giving you some money and telling you that if it costs you more, that he'd pay you back on his return. Would you trust that much? He did! The inn-keeper was a good neighbor, too. You see, no limits.

Would we be more like the Samaritan and the inn-keeper or more like the priest and the Levite? To what extent do we limit, that is, hold back our love? Do we have absolute limits? If so, we are <u>bigots</u>. Have we got floating limits? By this I mean that, given the circumstances, are we open to set them aside in order to let the love we all carry within come to the surface and shine like the sun? Jesus is the limit meter.

The Spirit of Christ keeps us from becoming bigots in the name of God. There are plenty of baptized Ku Klux Klanners; there are plenty of baptized white-hating African-Americans and Mexican-Americans, there are plenty of baptized gay-bashers, there are plenty of baptized INS agents who abuse the undocumented as in Arizona, and, in the name of God, they limit their love, failing to do what's right and compassionate.

Jesus' heart tells us: be compassionate, suffer with and respond to the people. How can we be a good neighbor in these economic times? Be peacemakers, be healers, be there for the suffering in whatever way you can, as imperfect as we are, but in the name of being with Christ in the least. Be the Samaritan if you feel called to do so; be the inn-keeper who risked to help another; be a healer of relationships; be a forgiver.

Can we approach the down-and-outers or touch the untouchables with love for Christ, who begs us to? Can we visit, feed, clothe, console, help reconcile, or just be there for whatever might be needed, even if it means holding a suicidal person in silence? Can we reach out and touch somebody's hand, and make this world a better place if we can? If yes, we are good neighbors, the real good-hands people. Sing with me, "Reach out and touch somebody's hand, make this world a better place, if you can…(repeat)…"

16th in ORD. TIME: Are we ready for the unannounced?

This famous Martha and Mary story is a classic example of what I have always told you to do: Read between the lines. Jesus is traveling <u>with</u> his disciples. He's not alone. So, what's really happening in this scene is Jesus and a group coming unannounced to the home of Martha, Mary and Lazarus, who is not named. Now, I'd like to ask the women in the congregation what you would do if your best friend came, unannounced into your home with a group of his or her friends?

Now I would ask the gentlemen in the crowd the same question: What would you do if your best friend came unannounced to your home with a group of his or her friends? Would you respond like Abraham in the 1st reading, getting Sarah to organize a feast for your friends? Would you become frantic, like Martha, acting just as she had been raised, treating the guest as if he or she were royalty?

Martha has been given the bum rap all of these years. She responds as the ancient teaching about the guest or the stranger: treat them as if sent by God. Look at the Abraham and Sarah story in the 1st reading, compare this with Martha. She drops everything to attend to their needs. Mary was neglecting her duties as a minister of hospitality by not helping Martha make sure that everything would be ready for the guests.

So why would Jesus respond as he did to his good friend Martha?

"A man trying to read the evening newspaper after coming home from a rough day at the office, is constantly interrupted by his children. One came and asked for money for an ice cream cone. He reached into his pocket and gave her the necessary coin. Another arrived in tears. Her leg was hurt and she wanted her daddy to kiss it and make it better. An older kid came with an algebra problem, and they eventually arrived at the right answer together. Finally, the youngest burst into the room looking for good old dad. The father said cynically, "What do you want?" The little one responded with, "Nothing, daddy! I just want to sit on your lap." (From "Living Smart," Dynamic Preaching, 1989, Pg. 5.)

If you were the father, which of these children would you feel best about? All of them love daddy, but which showed the kind of love a daddy and mommy would give anything for? Martha and Mary both love Jesus. Both show it in their own way. Jesus loves both Martha and Mary. But when Martha wants Mary to love Jesus as she does, Jesus says to Martha: "you are out of line, let her love me as she must."

Daddy loves each of his children and each loves daddy. Each child shows their love in a different way. Only the youngest shows daddy that he has no agenda but to sit in his lap where he feels loved and at home. Mary sits at the feet of Jesus, in the pose of the disciple, where she feels loved and at home. Martha feels at home doing the details of hospitality, even when Jesus doesn't demand or want it.

Jesus, unannounced, and can only hope for the minimum out of Lazarus, Martha and Mary. He didn't ask for a feast. He didn't ask Martha to do what she was doing. Mary finds herself at home at Jesus' feet. What's the better lot? The freedom to love, which Mary exhibits! Martha was not free to love Jesus, because she got lost in the details. Jesus wants us to come and sit in his lap while he is around. When he leaves, he says to us: Love one another as he has loved us. Simply put.

Are we free to love as we've been called to do? Are we free enough to let others love as they are called and are able to love? If we can answer yes, then we are ready to celebrate at this table. If we are not free enough to love and let love, then let us ask, as we break the bread of love and life, for the grace to be able to be free enough to love as we have been loved, and to let others love as they have been loved. May Jesus be able to say of us, "They have chosen the better lot."

17th in ORD. TIME: With prayer, change is on the way!

Over the years I've seen how many people choose to pray. I've seen centering prayer, when people repeat a word or phrase as a mantra. I've seen many pray the rosary which is a form of centering prayer. I've seen people use the scriptures to meditate. I've seen people use the scriptures and enter the scene as a cast-member. I've also seen how parents show their children to pray for others, a prayer we call intercessory prayer.

We just listened to how Abraham pleaded for the lives of those who lived in Sodom and Gomorrah. And we heard how Jesus showed the apostles how to pray as he prayed. What are the similarities and what are the differences in the styles of prayer?

Abraham and Jesus both converse with God with faith. Both are humble and simple. However, Abraham bargains with God for the lives of the 2 cities. This shows childishness. But, Abraham shows us just how much prayer changes God. God relented when Abraham pled.

Jesus, on the other hand, pleads in a different way, in a nearly-perfect prayer. Jesus knows God changes in a prayer relationship, but so does the Pray-er. Why? Because praying is being in relationship, in kinship, with our creator! Jesus calls God: Father. This is shocking because, to the Jews, God is totally other, so much so, that they didn't even pronounce God's name. Calling God Father meant that he and we are in relationship that is more kin than formal. So, think of "Kin-dom" of God, a kindom of familial relationships. Jesus shares God's will for the world: that God's kindom come. God's will to be done is for us be members of God's own kindom.

By saying "God's will be done," we submit our will to God's will, so that we think as God thinks, act as God acts, and love as God loves. Now we're ready to ask for what we need. We ask to be fed, to be nurtured with daily bread. It shows our total dependence upon God. Jesus' food was to do the will of the one who sent him: God. Our food is inextricably linked to doing what God would have us do!

We acknowledge we are weak and beg forgiveness for our sins, but Jesus puts a catch to it: <u>As we forgive those who sin against us.</u>

I find myself gulping as I say this, because I find it hard to forgive. Do you?

Forgiveness is learned. We're not born with the idea of forgiving those who harm us. We need role models. When I prepare couples for marriage I share if they ever have a disagreement in front of the kids, then reconcile in front of them, too. Another example is Dr. John Muyskens, who lived through WWII after witnessing the killing of his son. Then a 2nd son died in the war. He prayed for those who took his sons: 1st, because that's what Jesus would do; 2nd, because he knew praying changes the pray-er; and 3rd, prayer elevates us above the hate we might harbor. What a great teacher!

When we show we're above the hate this world can instill, God then takes delight and blesses us. There's no greater reason to pray than to connect so deeply with God that God loves and blesses us.

We learned prayer changes God through Abraham and that prayer changes the Pray-er through Christ. Now we discover that by changing ourselves, we change the world. How much more might we change humanity itself if we just learn to think well in love and blessing?

If we pray as if everything depends upon our praying, and work as if everything depends upon God's acting through us, we'll make a difference that we have lived at all. We will make God's kindom come and God's will be done. Prayer has power.

Jesus said: "Ask and it shall be given you; seek and you shall find; knock and it shall be opened to you…God will give the Holy Spirit to those who ask him." God's life is given to us. What more can we want?

18th in ORD. TIME: Hoard acts of kindness!

We heard: "Vanity of vanities, everything is vanity." Do we have vanity? Of course, we do. We all look to be happy, don't we? And at times our choices turn out badly don't they? Why? Vanity! If we can admit we make bad choices that lead us away from God, then we're vain. But it's tough to admit we are living in vain.

So many of us are afraid to lose what we have, that we turn to hoarding. If a water shortage is announced, watch what happens in the stores. Prices go up to take advantage of the buyer. The same happens with gasoline, with gas masks, with anything we deem a shortage of. I must say the illness of hoarding is pandemic here and abroad.

We're like the farmer, who had more than enough grain stored in his barns. Instead of giving away/selling the surplus, he tears down his barns and build larger ones. Yet, he never got to enjoy the fruits of his harvest. He could not ask the question: When is enough, enough? He loved things and used people, instead of loving people and using things. We have created idols out of things and money.

St. Ignatius, the patron-saint of discernment, said we are created to praise, reverence and serve almighty God, and in so doing save our souls. He also said something just as important. He said all things on this earth were created to help us save our souls, and to the extent that they help us do so, use them, and to the extent they lead us away from God, we are to discard or not use them. Do things lead us to God?

Only as a means to an end is what we have, valuable. It is worthless as an end in itself. To the driven by wealth, be it knowledge, property, money, or power, there's only 1 answer to, "When's enough, enough?" "Never!" To the balanced, who know the proper value of things, whose souls are intact, their answer is, "when the poor are no longer, and when all people who have, share with those who have not."

My father taught me the value of giving away in gratitude. When things were bad financially, he'd still line up envelopes in which he put money. 1st, was the one for the parish; then the ones for organizations that helped people. I once asked him why give away when we barely had enough for us to eat? He said, "Notice you said enough. When we have enough, it's a blessing from God. We are to give away what is more than enough. Do it and we'll be more blessed!" I've never forgotten it. That's why we tithe as a parish. We give away to good causes what is a bit more than enough to get by, and we are blest.

I thank God for my father and for St. Ignatius, because we priests can hoard as well. Some of us hoard degrees. Others of us, books, CD's, techno-gadgets, even computers. I have just moved and am amazed at the many boxes of stuff I've accumulated. My 1st project will be to open the boxes and give away what is useful, and throw away what's not. The ability to discern this comes from the gift of reflecting.

Now I am going to ask you to examine what you have and why you keep it, what you buy or buy into and why you buy or buy into it. If it leads you to God, by all means, keep and use it. If it doesn't, then give it all away. If you have closets/garages full of no-longer-used items or clothes, then give them to St. Vincent de Paul or the shelters.

If you have more money than you need, then look to your neighbors or your children or grandchildren and see what you can do for them. Maybe helping with a utilities bill will free a neighbor to pay one's rent/mortgage. Perhaps instead of buying a Mercedes SUV, consider an economy car and sending your child or grandchild to catholic school for years to come. Do not just react to life, reflect upon it and respond by deciding to let God show you the way. You will be blessed and find joy.

19th in ORD. TIME: Get our cargoes to heaven!

2 paddleboats were traveling side-by-side down the Mississippi from Memphis to New Orleans. Their sailors got into bragging. After the disses, they decided to race. One fell behind due to lack of fuel. They would have had enough for the normal trip, but not in a race. A sailor of the lagging boat decided to take the cargo and burn it as fuel. They won the race, but failed in their purpose: to deliver their cargo.

Max Lucado says of the story that we've been entrusted by God with cargo for the trip of life: our kids, spouses, friends. Our mission is to make sure the cargo is delivered to its destination. We must not forget: if we make our programs more a priority than the people in our life, they will suffer. How many people fail to reach their destination due to our forgetting the mission we accepted?

(Paraphrased from "Who will be crying at your funeral?" Dynamic Preaching, Vol. XIII, No. 3, pg. 30)

How we set our priorities shows what we really treasure in life. An easy way to discern where our treasure is: examine the 168-hrs. we have in a given week, and see how we spend our free time. To do this, we must 1st identify our "have-to-time" and free time. We have to eat, sleep, work, go to the bathroom, pay bills and taxes. On the average we spend about 130 hours doing "have-to" things. That leaves us 38 hours of free-to-choose time. Examine our use of this time and ask ourselves if you are pleased with the way the way you have chosen to use these hours.

It is this use of time that shows what we treasure most. What do we treasure? Let us compare our treasure with Jesus'? Jesus treasures our heart. Our hearts treasure what we have faith in, what we give our total self. It implies passion. Is our passion Christ's passion?

How we express our faith is learned. From whom did Jesus learn to express faith? From Joseph and Mary! But he also learned it in school. He learned what matters most is kin-ship, spending long hours feeding the relationships that mattered to him. He gave up carpentry to build a kindom of relationships. He left it for something better.

115

If our children are to learn what Jesus did, we must show them that God wants to be intimate with us. This education must become our main priority, but it's only shown in how we relate and nurture our relations.

I've seen people make some pretty bad choices. A bad choice is a refusal to discern, to examine what is of God and what isn't, what leads to God and what doesn't. We need the Holy Spirit's gift of discernment, yet we rarely pray for it, and when it comes, we haven't the faith to trust.

I treasure what I learned from my parents. They taught me how to love. They sent me and my 8 siblings to Catholic grammar/high schools. They wanted us to learn how to live in faith. We all learned this well. They gave us the ability to choose, but they wanted us to learn the values of our choices. They wanted their cargo to reach our destinations.

Our cargo is anxious to get to the promised-land, God's destination. How we get there is as important as getting there. Do we let the choices of others get in the way of our choices? Do we let ourselves be goaded into doing what is not in our best interest or that of our cargoes?

So, do we treasure our cargo and mission enough to put our whole heart into it because God is there? The fuel for the boat-ride, for the mission of getting our cargo to heaven, is the Eucharist and the other sacraments. Come, let us feed our holy paddle-boated souls and make sure our cargoes arrive. Let us show God we're proud of how we've used and are using our freely-chosen-time to make Christ's mission our own.

20th in ORD. TIME:
Conflict, an obstacle or an opportunity?

I've heard said that a prophet's job is to afflict the comfortable and to comfort the afflicted. Jesus was a source of conflict. What he taught divided his people. How he lived led him to be judged and condemned by the authorities, the comfortable; and to be praised by the people, who were afflicted by those authorities.

The sad part about a prophet is that one is not recognized as a hero or she-roe until after one's death. Most of them have been killed in history by those afflicted by their words. In our modern times we see Ghandi, Martin Luther King, Oscar Romero, Rutilio Grande, the sisters and Jesuits in Central America, were killed because they spoke the truth to those in power and comfort, and comforted those afflicted by them.

What does it take to be a hero/she-roe in God's eyes? Jesus told us that to be the greatest in the Kindom of God, one must hear the Word of God and keep it. He also said, "You are my friends if you do what I command you: love one another as I have loved you..." and, "as you forgive so shall you be forgiven;" and "come, blessed of my Father, and inherit the Kindom prepared for you from the beginning of time."

We are in the arena of life, and those in the stands cheering us on are those who went before us, those who heard the word and carried it out. They can't wait to welcome us at the finish line of a life well-lived. They are those who know we are imperfect and they don't care because they were imperfect. God wants us just as we are, to run the race and never give up. We're not in competition, but in communion. Would that we all cross the finish line and be cheered for having run!

Many of those who went before us suffered not knowing they had truly made a difference for having lived. They were welcomed for having run. We are called to build on what they did, and take the finish-line to new places, new heights of love and peace.

But there is still this notion of division. What is it that divides us, keeps us away from God and each other? Why do we avoid reflecting on and owning up to the answers to these questions?

Jesus, divides our complacency and categories of judging, to

117

show us how to reconcile with ourselves, our neighbor, and God. Jesus wants us to examine what makes us push people away, push God away, and to see the need to distance ourselves from what divides us.

Who do we push away? Which people? How about gays, people with HIV, of other religions, languages, or races? How about prostitutes, the homeless, mentally ill, down-syndrome people of all ages, divorced, single parents, people living together whatever their sexual orientation, feminists? How about queeny men, butchy women, youth with spiked hair or tattoos, drug addicts, and the list goes on? I know I've been guilty of these prejudices. But Jesus does not abandon them, or us.

Jesus constantly breaks through to cause conflict in each of us so that we may be one like Jesus and his Abba are one. I don't want you to think I'm advocating immoral behavior, now. I'm not. What I am saying is I'm not absolutizing society's or some of our Catholic's categories of exclusion. Jesus often made himself ritually unclean by associating with those pushed away so the good news of God's love could break through to the most hungry, thirsty, and love-starved of his day and our day.

What symbolizes working through conflict in order to grow and move on is the Eucharist. This is the table of universal fellowship, our breaking bread together no matter who we are or what we've done. Can we celebrate our dealing with the conflict Jesus sowed for the sake of our good, with gratitude? If so, let's break bread together with love. If still not yet, let's ask Christ to heal us so we might have the courage to walk with Society's unclean so that they may feel loved just as they are, just as we are, just as I am. That is turning conflict into an opportunity!

21st in ORD. TIME: Do not lose heart, discipline it!

"Do not lose heart when reproved by the Lord. For whom the Lord loves, the Lord disciplines." How did you feel to hear these words? I've thought about all the people who helped me learn to discipline myself. My parents, my grandparents, my teachers and coaches through the years, all taught me to reflect on what is needed to move forward and do well. It is how they taught what I will call, discipline.

Looking back, I can see God disciplined me through them all. Some did it well, and some over-stepped the bounds of decency, but all helped me learn. What I learned most was how to stop, reflect, then respond to a situation. Humans either react or respond to a stimulus. An animal solely reacts to stimuli by instinct. The ability to bypass reacting and responding is what separates us humans from being only an animal.

How would you rate yourself on the reaction/responding meter? Remember we are all members of the animal species. Hence, we all react from time to time. But do we always react? If so we're no better than an animal, who can't help but react. But if we have learned to stop, reflect, and then act, we have learned what discipline really is.

When I prepare young couples for marriage, I ask them to examine how their parents disciplined them. I have them identify the methods that worked and why they worked, and those that didn't work and why they didn't. It's then the couple can decide how both of them will be disciplining their children as partners in the task. It is then that the couple begins to be like God is with us.

What doesn't work for us is the kind of discipline that makes fun of us, puts us down, or strips us of our dignity. In other words, we hate being dissed, disrespected, no matter the reason behind the diss. We all hate to be yelled at, at *any* time, to be hit at *any* time, to be accused without facts, and to be prejudged for any reason whatsoever, right? Who likes to be humiliated? No one! Not even Jesus liked it, "...if I've spoken rightly, why do you strike me?"

It takes discipline to do our job well, to be a good student, to be a good son/daughter, a good mother/father, a good priest/ preacher, a good musician/singer, athlete/cook, a good doctor/

engineer. The best discipline does what's right so we learn to do the right thing. It comes from the heart, from the self that *knows* what needs to be done and how. To learn to do what's right, we need laws, commandments, rules, limits. They're part of the process of learning discipline.

Like Hebrews says: "At the time all discipline seems a cause not for joy but for pain, yet later it brings the peaceful fruit of righteousness to those who are trained by it." All my couples are able to identify the good discipline their parents used on them and the bad discipline. It's the difference between being humbled and being humiliated.

Youth grow up being *dissed* by almost everyone. Ask them. They're callused by the street-language in rap albums, movies, books, in class or the gym. They don't need to get it at home. But kids, the *dissing* you get isn't close to the *dissing* your parents get at work, the streets, the police, government offices, and even in Church. They protect you from the adult dissing that goes on. They, also, don't need to get it from you. They're not dumb or out of it. Ask them about what they go through to survive.

Share with and support each other. As Jesus says, the gate is narrow by which a Christian is to survive. We all go through phases that are burdens to others. So, help each other leave behind what keeps us from loving, respecting, and honoring one another.

Kids, love your parents. Parents, love your children. Church, love the people God sends your way by taking the *diss* out of discipline. Then we can say that we are truly entering by God's narrow door.

22nd in ORD. TIME: Be humble

Let me review what I said last week. We talked about removing the "dis" in discipline, meaning the type of external discipline which puts down, disrespects, or strips people of their dignity. We related this to the difference between humbling and humiliating. Today we must revisit the ideas, for Jesus said, "Those who humble themselves will be exalted, and those you exalt themselves will be humbled."

To humble yourself is to apply self-discipline, which means we don't always take "shotgun" to sit in the front seat of the car, or to jump in with an answer in class so that others can answer, or even if we got to church 1st, we don't take another's place as lector, Eucharistic minister, or soloist. It doesn't mean we can't do it, it means we choose not to, even if we can do it better. It shows the wisdom spoken of in the 1st reading.

Note the 1st reading: "the mind of a sage appreciates proverbs, and an attentive ear is the joy of the wise." Wow! This says that to be wise is to recognize wise sayings and listen to them. Listening is not the same as hearing. We all hear things, but we tend not to listen. Listening means to be attentive, focused on the other's words, not just planning to pounce with our own words. Humility means we consider what another is saying as truly important, even more so than our own thoughts.

Francis of Assisi said it best: "In all things preach the Gospel, and if necessary, use words." In other words, let our actions speak louder than our words, let our attitude shine through by what we do more than by what we say. That is true humility.

For those who consider themselves more important than another, the day of reckoning is coming. The exalted will be humbled. For those who consider others as more important and treat them such, you will be exalted. Such was Jesus' promise to us.

I've seen both things happen in and out of religious life, and in and out of the parish. Some who like to dominate discussions, classes, studies, eventually are put in their place, and the others stop listening to them. On the other hand, one who is silent, observing, and discerning, by the time one speaks, have the respect and people listen, exalting one's words as truth.

Jesus sees the poor, outcast and down-trodden as examples of who God finds important. In today's gospel we find the "Preferential Option for the Poor" most Christians and politicians disdain or neglect. Jesus is promising paradise to those who treat the poor as God's select. We call the service we give the poor: Social Justice, right relationship to those in need. To this we are all called.

Jesus will say: "My friend, come up higher!" if we heed his words in Matthew 25: "I was hungry and you gave me to eat; thirsty and you gave me to drink; naked and you clothed me; sick or in prison and you visited me... etc." Do this and you will also hear, "Come blessed of my Father, and inherit the kindom prepared for you since the beginning of time."

To carry this out takes humble faith, real hope, and genuine love. A faith that is humble is one that recognizes we are God's. It shows compassion, the response to God's words with our own words: "There because of the grace of God go I." And real love is the love that expects nothing in return. This kind of love sees the face of Christ in the lowly.

To be humble is to know who you are, whose you are, and for whom you are here on this earth. We are children of God, sent to love God and God's children, especially those who have no one to care for them. We are invited to the eternal banquet symbolized and signified by this banquet we share. We cannot pay God back for what we've received. God wants it that way. Give God the credit and give God, by way of the lowly, what belongs to God. Do this and we will be called to come higher.

23rd in ORD. TIME: God always gives us a 2nd chance!

If we study the world of the Bible more deeply, we would come to the conclusion that people in old times were not unlike us in our time. The difference is the kinds of cultures we live in. For example, biblical people lived in a culture that condoned having slaves. Today, we don't, but it wasn't so long ago that we did condone having them. I bring this up because Onesimus, mentioned in Paul's letter today, was Philemon's slave. He made Philemon angry due to taking one of Philemon's things.

Paul is begging Philemon to give Onesimus a 2nd chance due to his conversion to Christ. What is even more amazing is Onesimus' name means <u>useful</u>. Paul saw that Onesimus could be useful for the mission of evangelizing, and so he begged his friend to free him to serve.

Knowing this has made me think about the kind of God we have. Christ was killed by a society that did not give 2nd chances. After all, they were ready to stone the woman caught in adultery, and Jesus's apostles wanted to send down fire and brimstone on people who were healing in Christ's name without being a part of the band disciples. Jesus was just the opposite. He understood and cared enough to save them from harm.

Our God-with-us said, "Father, forgive them, for they know not what they do." To a rightly-condemned thief he said, "Today you shall be with me in paradise." He rewards U-turns in life and he advocates for the ignorant. Jesus would make a lousy police-man or woman. In fact, he would make a lousy, in-name-only Christian, or Jew, or any black-and-white religion.

Sometimes those around us are the biggest obstacle to receiving a 2nd chance. Why do I say that? Because we all know people who carry the name of Christ but without carrying the heart of Christ! Ask a divorced person, a gay person, a Black person, Mexicans, or people who look or sound different if they feel welcome in our country or in our church.

Returning to Philemon and Onesimus, can we see that St. Paul is testing the both of them? He was testing Philemon's conversion and Onesimus's discipleship. Were both carrying the heart of Jesus? What is the answer to the test question? Forgiveness! The true test of a Christian is his/her ability to forgive. After all, Jesus, in the prayer he taught us, says: "Forgive us our sins as we forgive those who sinned against us." He also said, "Forgive your enemies, those who harm you."

Mahatma Ghandi said, "The weak can never forgive. Forgiveness is the attitude of the strong." Are we strong enough to forgive? Are we strong enough to drop our absolute categories of judgment in order to have others a 2nd chance? St. Paul sent a letter advocating for his new disciple Onesimus to Philemon. He is showing us the ends to which he went to heal a relationship in order to free an on-fire disciple to do what he was called to do: bring Good News to the world.

Like Jesus said in his parable today, a plan is needed for those of us with difficulties forgiving, to effect the courage to forgive. We need to see the offender being blessed by Christ and by ourselves for days/weeks or months before meeting. We need to see ourselves calmly telling the culprit what he/she did and that we've forgiven them. Then we need to actually go and tell him/her that we have forgiven them.

As difficult as this is, this is what carrying our cross and carrying the heart of Christ is all about. Are we ready and willing? The choice is ours. If we choose wrongly, we can take solace in knowing that our God will always give us a 2nd chance.

24th in ORD. TIME: God loves us anyway!

"I once was lost, but now am found." The person who wrote this verse knew Christ intimately. The author of that phrase is the author of Amazing Grace. He was one of the lost sheep who was found by the Good Shepherd and brought back to the fold. He was once the lost coin who was later found and celebrated. He was one who discovered that God loves us no matter what we have done or have failed to do.

A close friend of mine recently retired after 40 years of faithfully shepherding patients as a nurse practitioner. Her practice threw her a retirement party to which I was invited to come and rejoice with my friend. Everyone, from the doctors to the office staff, came to honor her. It was obvious by the shared words and the tears that flowed, that she was deeply loved and respected, and would be deeply missed.

One attendee later called my friend to talk. She was deeply moved by how my friend was remembered, and yet deeply troubled at the same time. She was troubled by the thought of how she would be remembered by her co-workers and staff, and also by her family. She realized that if she were to retire tomorrow, probably very few would attend, and even fewer would speak out in her favor. She decided to change, to begin to make a difference as had been done in her.

She realized it's not too late to change, to make a difference in others that my friend had done for her. She once was lost, but now is found. That, my friends, is God shepherding us through the angels God sends our way. They could be family members or co-workers. They could be friends, coaches, teachers, mentors, or even the most un-loveable around us. Whoever they may be, the message of change is always the same: How do we want to be remembered when we retire or when we die? Are we living that way right now or not?

St. Paul was a murderer at worst and a persecutor of Christians at best. Yet, Christ hounded him through a prophet until Paul became the apostle to the Gentiles. He fell blinded, did what was told, and received new sight, one that found Christ in his fellow humans.

Catholic Digest tells of a child coming to her mom and asks, "Is God a grown-up or a parent?" Mom responded, "What's the difference?" The child boldly said, "A grown-up loves you when you're good. A parent loves you anyway."

(from "Why the Brit. Coast Guard doesn't like Eric, but God does, <u>Dynamic Preaching</u>, Vol. XVI, No. 3, pg. 62)

Some parents love their children only when they're good. To those kids God says, "Even if a mother forgets her child, I'll never forget you." A parishioner was clinically depressed for over 50 years, suffering from migraines for nearly 40. If anyone had reason to give up on God and life, she did. But she didn't.

Somehow, God's love gave her a reason to keep going, even when everything inside her told her to give up. Through her friends and her church, she's now healed of her depression, and her migraines are improving. She's now on fire with the love of God, looking for ways to share that love. Are we on fire for being found by the love of God?

We've all been or are lost sheep. God will never leave us alone until we're confronted with being found. At that point we must recognize the call to become shepherds like Christ was with us. Then, we're found. It is then we're made whole, for a real Christian carries out Christ's mission once it has been carried out in us.

Jesus wants us to know he loves us anyway. If we've been or are on drugs/alcohol, God loves us anyway. If we've had an abortion or helped procure one, God loves us anyway. If we've been a source of suffering for our families, even if they abandon us, God loves us anyway.

God's love for us doesn't depend on our being good; it's in God's character to love unconditionally. We can come close to loving like that, but only with God's help. Remember, there is more rejoicing in heaven for a sinner who realizes he/she is found, than for the 99 righteous who feel they have never been lost. Thank God, God loves us anyway.

25th in ORD. TIME: We were created to serve!

"We were created to praise, reverence and serve almighty God, and in so doing save our soul. Everything else was created to help us attain the goal for which we were created." (1st Principle & Foundation of St. Ignatius' Spiritual Exercises)

I was reminded of this when I read the Gospel. "Money is a means and never an end." Hence, if money interests us, remember it is a tool for the salvation of our souls. That's why Jesus said, "You can't serve God and money." God is an end; money is a means.

John Wesley, Methodism's founder, found it out through revivals and the great growth of his membership. His revivals attracted many a dysfunctional seeker. They felt moved to change from substance addicts to sober, hard-workers. They became so successful, their commitment to Christ and the church began to slip. They replaced their prior addictions with the addiction to making money.

Wesley found an amazing solution: earn all you can, save all come you can, and give all you can. Most of us can accept steps 1 and 2, but balk at the 3rd. Why? Because money is quite tempting and corrupting!

(Adapted from: "Financial Freedom," Dynamic Preaching, Vol. XXIII, No. 3, 2007, pg. 85)

Just look at the steward of the wealthy man's money in the gospel. Tempted by money, he made it his end & god. When caught defrauding and faced with losing his job and status, he took action and converted money into the means to a new future. This means insured his future and elevated his ingenuity to a commendation from Jesus.

Jesus commends him not for his fraud, but for creatively finding a solution to his soon-to-be-dire future. He made all he could, saved all he could, and now gave all he could to ensure gratitude from the receivers of his creativity: his boss' clients.

He took advantage of people and got caught. Isn't it amazing how necessity then became the mother of his invention?

It is that invention Jesus praises. He wants us to be just as creative and inventive. We're children of the light since Baptism. We're called to save our souls and use the things of this world to help us attain that end. Hence, we must make all we can, save all we can, and give all we can to help save others and ourselves, attaining oneness with God. That "all we can" is 1st and foremost, love. Then we can apply this to compassion, forgiveness, kindness, honesty, and any and all other virtues.

How we treat others will be the subject of our face-to-face account of our lives before God. Groups, institutions and individuals will be judged for this as well. How we individuals, families, churches, or nations treat each other, especially the poor, will be taken into account at our final judgment.

In the 1st reading Amos warns the bullies of the world, those bigger, stronger, wealthier and, in society's eyes, more powerful than others, and tells them, "Hear this, you who trample upon the needy, and bring the poor of the land to an end... I'll never forget any of their deeds." (Amos 8:4 & 7) Or the gospel: "Check yourself...you'll have to make an account of your service."

In other words: "Bullies, beware. Take a good look in the mirror." Are we honest with ourselves? Are we bullying others by using our intelligence, gifts, or strength to take advantage of them and hurt them?

God, through Amos and Luke, tells us we're called to be caretakers, stewards of those whom God has sent our way? The poor, the needy, the ignorant in things financial or in the practical art of living: all have been entrusted to us by God, to be responsible for them.

We must be stewards/caretakers, loving our neighbor no matter what. God also entrusts us to care for our lives, creation, animals and other humans. Make, save and give all we can to help us save our souls, which will be judged by how we serve what God has entrusted to us.

26th in ORD. TIME: I made you didn't I?

The Sufi master shared: "I found myself before a naked, hungry, sick child, shivering in the cold. I yelled at God: 'How can this be? Do something for him!' I went to bed with the of the memory kid's face. God's voice awoke me, "I did do something. I made you didn't I?" (Paraphrased from: "The Disabled Fox," The Song of the Bird, Anthony de Mello, Doubleday, 1982, pg. 79)

One difference between the Sufi master and Dives, the rich man in the Gospel, is the Sufi master noticed the poor boy, the Lazarus in his life, while Dives never noticed or cared that poor Lazarus lay outside his house. What God said to the master, God says to us, "I did do something (about poverty), I made you didn't I?"

There is something final and disturbing about the Gospel. At life's end we'll end up on one side of a huge chasm, our spiritual Grand Canyon. There's no crossing over once we're where we're supposed to be. One side is heaven, the other, hell. If you died right now, on what side of the chasm would you be?

We're challenged to think about this. We're given criteria for being sent to either side. 1st, hell: Amos tells those who take advantage of the helpless and hopeless poor, God will never forget their doings. So sins of <u>commission</u> can be a ticket to hell. Luke presents Dives, living high on the hog, ignoring Lazarus at his door. He's sent to hell for <u>not caring</u>, for doing nothing to help Lazarus, for sins of <u>omission</u>. Now you know why we say at Mass: "forgive me for what I've done and what I failed to do."

What an idea! If we do nothing for our neighbor, if we don't care, we'll go to hell. Don't get me wrong: having wealth isn't a sin. What matters is what we do with it. This passage shocked Jesus' people, because wealth meant being blessed by God, and poverty meant being punished by God. Jesus flips this notion: the poor, like Lazarus, will go to heaven; the rich, who act like Dives, will go to hell. It's that simple.

Do you remember: "Blessed are the merciful for they shall obtain mercy?" Apply it to this notion: "blessed are you wealthy, who put your wealth at the service of the poor, for the kindom of heaven is yours." What a notion for developing nations!

129

I took a class in Zen Buddhism, which fascinated me. I received some insights from the Buddhist way of thinking. There is an 8-fold path to alleviate the suffering in the world: right views, right intention, right speech, right action, right livelihood, right effort, right mindfulness, and right meditation. The Bible needs only one step: right relationship, which includes the eight! Right relationship is what <u>justice</u> is in the Bible.

Was it right for Dives not to help Lazarus when he could? No! Is it right for us not to help the poor of the world when we can? No! It is obvious throughout Luke's Gospel that God has a preferential option for the poor. In other words: if our love for God and neighbor doesn't include love of the poor, then we're not one with God.

Now don't mistake my words for advocating giving pure hand-outs! That's not what I am saying. I'm saying we need to find out why the poor are poor and help them out of poverty. Some of us need to feed or clothe them, while others need to advocate before the powerful to help change the structures that keep them poor. And still others of us need to help the poor get out of their poverty. These are the 3 points of the Right Relationship Triangle of Social Justice: direct service, advocacy, and empowerment.

We've been challenged. It's our choice. We can be like Dives and end up on the wrong side of the chasm. Or we can be like the Sufi master and do something for the Lazarus's all around us, and stand side-by-side with Lazarus and Christ on the right side of the chasm. God made us to do something for those who can't do <u>for</u> themselves <u>by</u> themselves. Are we up to it?

27th in ORD. TIME: Faith is a verb!

How many of you think belief is the same as faith? It isn't! Many people believe in God, but have no faith in God. The devil believed Jesus was God's son, but surely he had no faith in him. Belief as assent says, "I believe in God." Belief as faith commitment, says, "I believe in God, and so I give myself to God, the Lord of my life." See the difference? Belief is just noun, faith is a dynamic verb.

Our readings call us to faith. Faith begins with a spark, an ah-ha moment. A spark starts a fire, but faith needs to be fanned just like a flame if a fire is to burn, and fanning takes work. We received the spark at Baptism. It was fanned at Confirmation and 1st Communion. That's what sacraments do: they fan the flame of faith, which needs them to keep burning like a fire in our belly. That's why we come to Mass!

And, you know, fires know no fear. They just go. People of real faith just go as well. "God did not give us a spirit of timidity, but a spirit of power, of love and of self-discipline." Paul is telling us we've had hands imposed on us for the purpose of giving us the Holy Spirit. We cannot be shy or timid about our faith, but we are. Why?

When faith is mistaken for belief, fear can take over. But when we have real faith, the power of love is in our hearts. Paul, like Jesus, had the power of an extraordinary purpose: to preach Christ with fire in his belly. Jesus' was to preach Good News to the poor, return sight to the blind, free the oppressed, heal the sick, and announce God's favorable year. Paul accepted the same mission but not until he left behind his previous one: persecuting Christians. What prior missions must we leave behind to take Christ's?

Once Paul did, he became a power-driven preacher, one whose power came from God. People of real faith are driven by love. Love has the transforming power to focus our mission. Is our love about mission or about us? Is it about the served or the server?

Love focuses, but self-discipline keeps our eyes on the prize. One can have the greatest mission on earth, but without the self-discipline to stay focused, our mission will flounder, even fail. Many have great missions, but lack the self-discipline to do it.

The Society of Jesus, also known as the Jesuits, is the group Pope Francis and I belong to. Did you know we form the largest Missionary Order in the Church? Most people know us by our colleges and high schools, but we really are an Order of missioned men. Every one of us is missioned, meaning sent, meaning being apostles. Our provincial sends us to promote a faith-that-does-justice. We learn self-discipline so as to survive and thrive where many fear to tread.

A Jesuit friend shared a story told him on a woman's death bed: "I now know the meaning of life! As a child and teen, we serve; in our 30's and 40's, we serve; in middle-age, we serve; in our 60's, 70's and retirement, we serve; when we're sick, or dying, and on our last day of life, we serve." "I came to serve and not be served," said Jesus, and that service may never be noticed. Faith need not be noticed. Belief needs to be noticed. Belief is about the server; faith is about the served.

"We walk by faith and not by sight," says the Scriptures. To walk by faith is to serve, and to serve is a verb. If and when we serve out of faith, coming from a love seeking justice, that is, right relationship, we shall hear one day, "Come, good and faithful servant, and inherit the kindom prepared for you from the beginning of time...Come share my joy."

28th in ORD. TIME: I want to be seen!

"Religion isn't (just) a set of beliefs, ... of prayers or of rituals. Religion is 1st and (mainly) a way of seeing. It can't change the facts about (our) world, but it can change the way we see those facts, and that, ... can make a difference."

(adapted from "Finishing in the top 10%," Dynamic Preaching, 1998, Vol. XIII, no. 4, pg. 12-13)

In one of my favorite movies, Avatar, the characters use the words, "I see you," to mean: "I see you for who you really are, and I love you." Every one of us desires to be seen, to be noticed, and to be cherished for who we really are; right? Yet, we came here today with many things on our mind, but none of them included really seeing each of us.

Rabbi Harold Kushner's book: Who needs God, speaks of seeing:

The late Leo Buscaglia wrote about making that difference: "The purpose of a human is to matter, to make a difference that we've lived at all." To make a difference means that someone notices and gives witness to what we have done. We all want people to notice and to be respectful of us as human beings, and not treat us as things to be feared or avoided. The epitome of exclusion due to fear was a leper in Jesus' day, or, in our day, a street-person with AIDS or SARS.

But it doesn't take much for us to feel we've lost our dignity. Our parents/teachers can say things at times that make us feel isolated or demeaned, even without knowing they had. Our best friends can say things at times that hurt us badly. Sometimes even our pastors, sisters, or religious, can shock us by their lack of compassion or tact. And even here, in 2013, governments & churches are targeting gays, immigrants, Muslims, and the homeless as not worthy of respect. So, we come here to find a sense of community, acceptance and purpose.

The lepers built a sense of community based on a common illness. Never mind that Jews and Samaritans hated each other, they came together due to a common enemy: leprosy. However, they wanted to be whole, and so they asked Jesus for mercy and got much more. Jesus heard their pleas, dealt with them like human beings, and sent them to show their priests they'd been healed. To these men, hungry for contact and kindness, hungry to belong again, Jesus returns their dignity. They can go back to their homes, synagogues, and towns. They can walk about, be touched and touch, without fear of being excluded or derided. The Samaritan leper was made whole, and he showed gratitude and discipleship. His healing broke the wall of religious separation.

Are there parts of our lives in which we feel excluded or derided? Are we part of the people who exclude or deride? If so, then we need to ask Jesus for mercy here and now. We already did it in the Penitential Rite, but now that we've better identified our need to heal or be healed, perhaps we can ask Jesus for mercy and compassion.

For what might we need God's mercy/compassion? Perhaps we're carrying the burden of un-forgiveness. Perhaps we're not proud of our bodies, minds, or souls. Perhaps we've procured or helped procure an abortion. Perhaps we've lied to someone, or had an affair. Perhaps we're addicted to alcohol, drugs, pornography, food or gambling. Maybe we're workaholics. Maybe we're homo or immigrant-phobic. God promises to be with us always, even in the midst of lost dignity or sin. Can we trust God's promise and seek mercy?

Jesus will send us all, like he did the 10 lepers, to be healed "On the Way," on His Way. The word "Eucharist" means Thanksgiving. Might we be grateful for what God has done, is doing and will do for us?

Jesus points to a grateful Samaritan, showing his awe of gratitude. May we be singled out in the heavenly court for truly living a grateful life and in turn make a difference for having lived and loved. Can we get in touch with what God has done, is doing, and will do for us? Can we respond by leaving here today as God's apostle?

29th in ORD. TIME: Faith is lived.

The New Colossus

Not like the brazen giant of Greek fame,
With conquering limbs astride from land to land;
Here at our sea-washed, sunset gates shall stand
A mighty woman with a torch, whose flame
Is the imprisoned lightning, and her name:
Mother of Exiles. From her beacon-hand
Glows world-wide welcome; her mild eyes command
The air-bridged harbor that twin cities frame.
"Keep ancient lands, your storied pomp!" cries she
with silent lips. "Give me your tired, your poor,
your huddled masses yearning to breathe free,
the wretched refuse of your teeming shore.
Send these, the homeless, tempest-lost to me,
I lift my lamp beside the golden door!"

By Emma Lazarus, on the Statue of Liberty

We just heard read: "When the Son of Man comes, will he find faith on the earth?" Is Jesus frustrated? Yes! His message isn't getting across. He's frustrated seeing his disciples depend solely on him, and not on the Father who sent him. He wants them to learn how to pray and then act.

Jesus exalts a persevering woman before an unjust judge. Knowing who and how he is, she persists in seeking justice. She's like those described on our Statue of Liberty: the tired, poor, and wretched refuse. The judge is like those to whom the poem and the parable is directed: to the rich and powerful throughout history.

Like the Mother of the Exiled, she's a she-roe for those who strive for justice: immigrants, gays, women, the working poor, and community organizations like PACT and the Interfaith Council for Worker Justice. She didn't give up, and her reward was justice that came from a judge who normally wouldn't care about her. Do we persevere like that? Do we even know what justice means so as to persevere in asking for it?

If injustice happens to us or around us, do we react or respond? A reaction is an immediate, un-reflected action. A response is a slow, discerned action after stopping, praying, and then acting. If evil happens do we move forward or do we give up? When life gives us a lemon, do we throw it away or do we make lemonade and share it with the world? Life is not over just because it didn't turn out like we planned. Life never turns out like we planned! So What? Get over it and move on!

We've been looking deeply at faith over the past 4 weeks. We now know that faith is a verb and not a noun, it is action based on belief. It is a partnership with the God who created us. Justice is right-relationship not fairness. It implies we're right with God, the universe, and each other. The partnership implies being sent, but discernment, which feeds the partnership and prepares us to be sent, implies prayer.

Some think prayer's a waste of time. So what? Do it anyway! Prayer changes God, changes the prayer, and changes the way we look at the world. Isn't that worth doing? Pray as if everything depends upon us and act as if everything depends upon God and our faith will bear fruit.

We've all heard life's not fair? Well, prayer helps us cope when life's not fair. Life is like the unjust judge, and prayer, like the poor woman, results in a reward for the persevering. If we pray for change in life and it doesn't, it changes how we look at life and accept it as it comes. What we can't control is God's. This reduces stress, and keeps us healthy.

Listening in prayer shows us what to do with what we can control. God will show us how to love and live better. God tells us to do the right thing always, do the loving thing in everything. There is no greater joy than knowing we have loved and are loved.

Can we love life as it comes, without comparing it to others? Do we pray each day to make a difference for having lived? If so, then the Son of Man will find faith in us, and be overjoyed.

ALL SAINTS DAY: Are our lives lanterns?

I'd like to know how many of you are ready to be inscribed in our Book of the Dead? Come now! Raise your hands who are ready. As you can see, few of you are really ready to meet God face to face. Why? Why aren't you ready? What's keeping you from being ready?

We celebrate All Saints Day, the day God gives thanks for the lives of those inscribed in the Book of Life. It's a great Church Feast. We remember with love all of our saints: those canonized, not-canonized and our living saints. Those who are canonized are the classics, those on the stained-glass windows, whose biographies we all know. The non-canonized are those who have lived holy lives, but will never be formally canonized as heroes. The living saints are those who deserve to be imitated for how they are living their lives right now.

In other words, they are heroes/she-roes to their families, their neighborhoods, their work places, their nations, and their churches. There is a restaurant in Wyoming that has a sign that reads: "A hero is someone who turns on a great light in the world, who serves as a lantern in the dark streets of life so that others may be guided by them. A saint is a man or woman who walks through life's dark paths, and whose very person is the light."

Saints are people worthy of emulation. They have an integrity that lets them remain firm when the world asks for something different. To be a saint is to have a special way of living. It is also to be a witness to what Christ has done in one's life and a witness to God's presence. When ones pilgrimage through life ends, the saint has left a better world for having lived.

Anthony de Mello, a Jesuit, tells a story about a man who is so holy that the angels sing for joy at just seeing him. What's interesting is he has no idea that he is holy. He lives his life emanating goodness like a flower sharing its fragrance and beauty, or a candle its light. His holiness consists in this: "He forgets someone's past and looks only at today. He looks beyond appearances and sees the core of each being, where innocence will not let him see what another is doing. That's how he can love and forgive everyone. He never believes he is doing the extraordinary. That's how he treats all people. (Ibid., pg. 13-14)

The life trajectory, the vital attitude of a Christian person must be this: To want to leave the world a better place for having lived at all. Being a saint is a way of living, a way of witnessing to the presence of Jesus in the world, living so that the world can become a better place. Christ calls us to live with mercy, peace, justice, and generosity, all of which lights up the darkness.

Today we celebrate and remember the lives of those who served as lanterns of bright light in our world of darkness. Today we share with our loved ones what we remember about our loved ones, so that their memory never dies. Today we speak of saints, whose lives make them worthy of being imitated.

Let us ask for the grace to leave this world better for having lived in it. Let's ask for the grace to see beyond appearances and see someone as God does: with love and forgiveness. Let's ask for the grace to learn to give our lives in service of others, and thus leaving a better-lit place to live.

30th in ORD. TIME: Teach like the Master!

Years ago I heard an expression that's dead-wrong: "Those you can, do, and those who can't, teach." Believe this and we call Jesus a fraud.

In *A man for all seasons*, Thomas More beckons Richard Rich, "Be a teacher. You're a great teacher." "But who knows I am a great teacher?" asked Richard. "Your students, yourself, and God! Not a bad company, I must say."

Again we see the theme of teaching prayer highlighted by Jesus in his famous parable of the Pharisee and the Tax-collector. Jesus wants to teach his people to pray humbly. So why teach? Let's see about why.

"I'm a teacher. I was born the moment a question leapt from the mouth of a child. I've been many people in many places. I'm Socrates exciting the Athenian youth to discover new ideas through questions. I'm Anne Sullivan tapping the secrets of the universe on Hellen Keller's hand. I'm Aesop, Hans Christian Anderson, Jesus, revealing truth using countless stories.

I'm Marva Collins fighting for every child's right to an education. I'm Mary McCloud Bethune building a great college for my people, using orange crates for desks. I'm the names of those whose names ring like a Hall of Fame for humanity: Booker T. Washington, Buddha, Confucious, Ralph Waldo Emerson, Leo Buscaglia, Moses, Jesus, and many more.

Throughout the a typical day I've been called upon to be an actor, friend, nurse and doctor, coach, finder of lost articles and lost spirits, a money lender, a taxi driver, psychologist, substitute parent, salesperson, politician and keeper of the faith.

Material wealth is not one of my goals, but I am a full-time treasure seeker in my quest for new ways my students can use their talents, talents that sometimes lie buried in self-defeat.

I'm the most fortunate of all who labor. A doctor ushers life into the world in one magic moment. I see life reborn each day with new questions, ideas, and friendships. An architect knows if one builds with care, one's structure may stand for centuries. A teacher knows if one builds with love and truth, what one builds will last forever. I am a teacher... and I thank God for it every day."

(Adapted from John W. Schlatter's: "I am a teacher" in <u>Chicken Soup for the Soul</u>, pg. 145-147)

What one builds as a teacher will last forever. Who doesn't want to know that one's labor will last forever? We're called to build something that lasts, to bear fruit that lasts. In today's parable of the Pharisee and the tax-collector, Jesus, the teacher, tells us: "act justly, love tenderly, and walk humbly with God," (Micah 6:8) which builds something that lasts.

A Pharisee was seen as holy because he obeyed the letter of the law. This made him righteous. He was a good person, I'm sure, but he lacked what's important. By boasting to God, he lacked humility. By putting down the tax-collector, he lacked justice, and by condemning sinners, he lacked compassion and tender love.

He did things right, but did not do the right thing, the just thing. He gave tithes on all he earned, but he gave to be noticed and not from a loving, compassionate heart for the betterment of the world. He fasted more than required, but not to purify his mind, body and spirit. So, "What good is it to gain the whole world and lose oneself doing it?"

And so, we're left with Jesus telling us, like St. Thomas to Richard Rich: <u>be a teacher</u>. Teach others to <u>act justly</u> at home or work, in & out of Church, in our neighborhoods, for acting justly treats creation, each other, and oneself as God's own gifts of self to us. Teach others to <u>love tenderly</u>, meaning not possessively, manipulatively, or just erotically. And teach others to <u>walk humbly</u>, not humiliatedly, with God.

Let us obey God's law to love each other as we have been loved. Let us teach by example, sharing so others may live and learn from us. Let us teach by giving without expectation of return. Let us teach by being humble, sharing and walking with each other and thus walking with God. Who will know we're good teachers of Gods way and law? Christ tells us: "My children, myself, and God, not a bad company I must say."

31st in ORD. TIME: Solve the puzzle that is us!

All of us have worked on puzzles. When we open the box, we see many pieces and we wonder if we can figure it out. To help us, the author of the puzzle gives us what it will look like when we solve it. Then begins tough part: that of putting each piece in the right place to help us match the image.

Think of God as the author of the puzzle that is us. To help us put ourselves together, God sent us the image of who we are to be: Jesus the Christ. The puzzle box is the Bible. And today we have the image of God who loves and forgives us, hoping that we can repent, which means looking at our life anew and letting ourselves be changed by that re-look. Our box has three main pieces: knowing who we are, whose we are, and for whom we have been created to love and serve as Christ loves and served us.

That's exactly what happened to Zacchaeus. His life had been diverted from the real Zacchaeus to a greedy tax-collector who worked for the enemy: the Romans. No one in town thought much of him. In fact he was public enemy #1 to them. Then he hears about the amazing Jesus, who is coming to his town. He goes up a tree because he was too short to see over the great crowds. Before he could say anything, Jesus calls him by name. "Oh my God, he knows who I am!"

On top of that, Jesus invites himself to dine at his house. Excitedly, he comes down and runs home to prepare to receive the surprise of his life. He hears the taunts at Jesus for choosing to socialize with the enemy. So he tells Jesus he will give what he has saved to the poor and pay back all those he defrauded 4 times over. That's restitution and real repentance. Zacchaeus, the unacceptable, is transformed by Christ's love and forgiveness into who he was meant to be. So, what does this mean for us?

We, too, have been called by name at Baptism. We are given the image of Christ by the Holy Spirit, who abides in us from that moment. We're given Bibles, rosaries, a candle, and a white garment, to remind us of our real-selves-to-be. We must read about Jesus and become like him. We must pray and stay in contact with the God, who reminds us to be a child of the light. We must witness to who we are, whose we are, and for whom we are here.

Rev. Angela Askew is clear: "What Jesus showed Zacchaeuss is that God accepts and transforms the unacceptable, loves the unloveable, & forgives the un-forgivable."

(Adapted from "A small man who was given a big heart," <u>Dynamic Preaching</u>, Vol. XXVI, pg. 25-26)

We, like Zacchaeus, are invited to live a faith-that-does-justice.

Have our lives become unacceptable/unlovable in some way? Has the image of our being become distorted by our actions or inactions? Do we know who we are, whose we are, and for whom we are here on earth? The Gospel's message should console us. If we can realize, like Zacchaeus, that God loves us and calls us to be who we were meant to be, then we have the chance to change what needs to change to match the image.

When we break bread together, we put more pieces of our puzzles' image together. Join me in asking Jesus for the grace to work for the transformation and acceptance of the unacceptable in us and the world. We're called to be lovers, peacemakers, careers. We must show love for our enemies, the un-loveable; we must make our home a haven of peace. And we must care: for our universe, water, resources, land, each other, and ourselves. In learning to care, we forgive ourselves for the sins we've committed or for the good we failed to do. In learning to care, we put more pieces of our truer being into the puzzle that we are meant to be.

Let us leave here today as apostles who work to accept and transform the unacceptable, who love the unlovable, and who forgive the unforgivable. Let us be apostles-for-others who live a faith-that-does-justice! Do this and those parts of us that are unacceptable, unlovable, and un-forgivable will all be healed, and the image on the Box of our puzzle that remains will be the <u>WE</u> God meant us to be. Now, isn't that worth celebrating?

32nd in ORD. TIME: The cross: can you get up on it?

Two men baptized at the Easter Vigil felt overjoyed to be welcomed as new Catholics! A year later, both attended Good Friday's service. One asked the other, "Would you get up on the cross with Jesus?" He said, "I can make it up to the cross, but not get up on it." What they addressed is martyrdom, being a witness to our faith. It takes time to get there.

It made me think: "For what am I ready to give my life? Does knowing I will rise make a real difference to me or not? Do I fear dying? On what is that fear based?" I begin my All Saints/All Souls homily with the same idea each year. I ask, "How many of you are ready to be inscribed in the Book of Remembrance?" It saddens me how few put up their hands. I say, "Once again you failed the final exam! I asked are you ready to be inscribed? Not, do you want to be inscribed?"

The theme of the Gospel is faith. We know faith is God's gift. It gets us up. It gives meaning to our living and dying, and it makes us want to grow. For us with faith, no explanation of what happens at death is necessary. For the faithless, no explanation is enough. Do we believe we'll have life after death or not? Our lives witness to our answer.

Jesus' today reveals that heaven exists, there's no marriage there, and we'll recognize each other. Our love for God and neighbor will grow to an unimaginable size. This revelation should console a person of faith. Does it console us enough to remove our fear of dying? To the faithless, none of this matters enough to change. Fear will always be there!

But even people of faith fear death. Why? It's the great unknown. No one has returned to share what's on the other side, not even Lazarus, who spent 4 days in the great beyond. There's no news at 11 to tell us what's what on the other side. Jesus didn't reveal what happens after death, but what is to come: paradise. What we learn about heaven or hell, we learned in his parables, like today.

We've all watched the late-night commercials that try to sell us the latest gadgets. It cracks me up to hear, "you can get all this for $19.95." But what always gets me is, "Wait, there's more!" So it made me think about teaching the Gospels that way. Imagine me saying at the end of what I'm offering, "But wait, when you die, there is more!"

What might remove the fear of death in us? In St. Ignatius Loyola's spiritual exercises there's a meditation a retreatant makes on one's own death. Imagine where you go at the moment of death and who's there. Without analyzing, what happens? I was given the gift of knowing that, despite my sins, I was loved, forgiven and called to serve. As my fear of death left me, I embraced my vocation of being a Jesuit priest. Go home today and try this. Note what happens to you in it?

You can't imagine how freeing it is to know you will be with God! It freed me to be excited about living and dying both. I'm excited when I awake because I've been given one more day to love, to show compassion, to make a difference for having lived. The thought of not waking up gladdens me because I'll be sharing eternity with our Lord.

You will never really live until you are at peace with your death. I learned this 34 years ago at St. Joseph's Hospital in Phoenix, in their Oncology, Life Enrichment Program. Sr. Madonna Marie who trained us wouldn't let us on the floor with a patient or the family until we were at peace with dying. The result is I can be peacefully present to you all in the most difficult moments of your family's life and to walk with you.

Might you learn it today? What will it take to free you enough to be peacefully and totally present to all of life and all of death? Embrace the answer so that when you hear the question, "Would you get up there on the cross with Jesus?" you can fearlessly and faithfully answer with all your heart, "Yes, by all means, bring it on!"

33rd in ORD. TIME: Go M.A.D., y'all!

St. Paul and Jesus didn't appreciate seeing busybody or idling disciples. Neither did he enjoy seeing those who wouldn't do their share of the work. Paul said,

> "On the contrary, in toil and drudgery, night and day we worked, so as not to burden any of you... Rather, we wanted to present ourselves as a model for you, so you might imitate us. In fact, when we were with you, we taught you if anyone was unwilling to work, neither should one eat. We hear some among you are conducting themselves in a disorderly way, by not keeping busy but minding other's business." (2 Thess. 3:7-12)

Humanity's history is filled with people who work and those who take the credit. Remember when we would be given school project that involved having partners? One would inevitably do all the research and much of the hard work, and the other would be the smooth-talking, credit-taking partner. Most of us would let it go to keep the peace, but, inside, we were angry, right? Pope John XXIII, in an interview was once asked how many people worked in the Vatican. He answered, "About half."

We can laugh, but Christ hated lukewarm disciples. "I'd rather have you hot or cold. Lukewarmness makes me sick to my stomach." But, why? He knew nothing destroys the sense of community more than the lukewarm. They do more harm than good because they tend to criticize workers and avoid the reminder of their idleness.

A pastor, Ron Hutchcraft, once made a great suggestion that I feel can cure the sins of idleness/lukewarmness: Jesus wants us to Go M.A.D. That may sound like a crazy saying, until you unpack the meaning of M.A.D. It stands for "Make A Difference."

Hence, we, who claim Christ as our Lord and Savior, have some homework to do: Go and Make a Difference, Go M.A.D. for Christ.

(Paraphrased from: "A Faith that Works," Dynamic Preaching, Vol. XXIX, No. 4, pg. 40-41)

We have celebrated and are celebrating in the month of November the models for our lives, our saints. They are both canonized saints and un-canonized saints. We also have living saints that show us how to live our lives. In other words, they are models of people who did Go M.A.D.

As we prepare to celebrate the feast of Christ the King next Sunday, we must look at ourselves closely and ask if others could use the way we live our faith as people gone M.A.D. for Christ. Are we heroes and she-roes for others to imitate and be like?

Today's Gospel brings a reality check into our thoughts, however. We will go through hardships in the name of Christ if we decide to Go M.A.D. in a world that doesn't want to hear Good News. We'll have heartaches, we'll have losses, we'll all miss the mark. None of these, however, should discourage us from going and making a difference. A dream is a mental goal that helps motivate us to make it happen, but if we don't focus or train, if we lack the discipline to go make a difference that we have lived, we'll never be models of apostleship like Paul was.

An apostle is a teacher of life who learned through a period of discipleship. We're all called to be disciples 1st and apostles 2nd. We all come to Mass as disciples, as learners of God's Word and will. We leave Mass as apostles, as teachers sent to apply what we've learned. We've learned that God asks us to give our all, to Go M.A.D. for God. Are we up to the task?

CHRIST the KIN:
Does our heart contain Christ's heartbeat?

In the 1993 movie, In the line of fire, a Secret Service agent is grieving for not being able to step in the line of fire of the assassin's bullet meant for Kennedy 30 years prior. He's facing a similar situation: "taking a bullet for the president." The moment comes and he steps in the line of fire, just as he was trained. He knew the value of saving the president for the people, and so he fulfilled his duty.

On Calvary we have a role-reversal. It is God who recognizes the value of us, and steps in the line of fire so that we might live. It is on the cross that we see how valuable we are to God.

(Paraphrased from, "The king who died," Dynamic Preaching, Vol. XXII, No. 4, 2007, pg. 56)

All of us say we are created in the image and likeness of God. But we live not believing it. For, if we lived like we really believed it, we wouldn't treat others the way we do, for they, too, are God's image. By sending Christ to the earth, God says: "I love you more than you know. I love you enough to send my son to show you how to live and love." The cross is the sign of that love, and it is the sign of our calling to do for others as God has done for us.

A girl was swimming at the beach, unaware of the strength of the current. By the time she realized she couldn't touch bottom, she cried for help. A man heard her and dived in to help. He knew to swim parallel to the shore until there was no more force of current. The girl was trembling partly from the cold, partly from exhaustion, and partly from fear. She said, "Thank you, sir, for saving my life." He said, "Don't mention it. Now live your life as if it were worth saving."

The cross is the sign of God telling us: "Live your lives as if they were worth saving, which they are." I hope that all of us, each time that we make the sign of the cross, recognize that, when we do, God saved us and wants us to live as if we believe we were saved. In other words, we must live our lives in the way we want to be remembered, like the girl will remember the man who saved her.

In Dec. 1997, a youth took a gun to school and killed 7 fellow students. The parents rushed to school with the prayer that their child be safe. One mother received the bad news. Despite the grief and the pain, when she was asked by the hospital for permission to use her son's organs, she said, "Yes." Months later she discovers that her son's heart was given to a Pastor. She called and they agreed to meet. They prayed in thanksgiving for her son's life. Before leaving she asked to put her ear to his chest to hear her son's heart beating one last time. (ibid. Pg. 59)

When God wants to hear Christ's heartbeat, God puts his ear to our chest. He's overjoyed when he hears Christ's heartbeat. Is Christ in us or not? What needs to happen to prove his presence? We must live as if we were worth saving or live as we want to be remembered for having lived. That will be proof enough for God.

All life is valued by God. What must we do to believe this? Well, we must treat others, no matter their situation/appearance, as if God were that person. That's what it means to live justly. That is what it means to live like Christ, who calls us to do as he did.

Blessed Miguel Agustín Pro, S.J. was killed by a firing-squad on Nov. 23, 1927. He was falsely accused of plotting to kill the president of Mexico. With arms outstretched like a cross, and with rosary in hand, he stepped into the line of fire of the squad crying out, "Viva, Cristo Rey...Long live Christ the King!"

Should the occasion present itself, would we be able to do as he did? Only if our heartbeat contains that of Christ, would we be able to answer yes! If and when we can answer "yes" will we hear like the good thief, "Today you will be with me in paradise."

BIBLIOGRAPHY

AUTHOR	PUBLISHERS/TITLES
Aurelio, John R .	CROSSROAD, New York Gather Round, Christian Fairy Tales for all ages, 1982 Fables for God's People, 1988 Colors, Stories of the Kingdom, 1993
Ausubel, Nathan	CROWN PUBLISHERS A Treasury of Jewish Folklore, 1948
Bausch, William J.	TWENTY THIRD PUBLICATIONS Storytelling Imagination and Faith, 1984 Timely Homilies, 1990 Telling Compelling Stories, 1991 More Telling Stories,Compelling Stories, 1993 Story Telling the Word, 1996 A World of Stories, For Preachers and Teachers, 1998
Bennett, William J.	SIMON & SCHUSTER, Rockefeller Center, NYC The Book of Virtues, 1993
Bruchac, Joseph	FULCRUM PUBLISHING, Golden Colorado Native American Stories, 1991
Buber, Martin	SHOCKEN BOOKS, New York Tales of the Hasidim, Early Masters, 1947

Burghardt, S.J.,   PAULIST PRESS, New York
Walter   Grace on Crutches, 1986
                       Lovely in Eyes Not His, 1988
                       Preaching: The Art and the Craft, 1987
                       Seasons That Laugh or Weep, 1983
                       Sir, We would Like to See Jesus,
                       Still Proclaiming Your Wonders, 1984
                       Tell the Next Generation, 1980
                       To Christ I look, 1989
                       Dare to be Christ, 1991
                       When Christ Meets Christ, 1993
                       Speak the Word with Boldness, 1994
                       Love is a Flame of the Lord,
                       Let Justice Roll Down Like Waters, 1998

Canfield, Jack &   HEALTH COMMUNICATIONS, INC.
                       Deerfield Beach
Hansen, Mark Victor   Chicken Soup for the Soul,
                       A 2nd Portion of Chicken...,
                       A 3rd Portion of Chicken...,
                       A 4th Portion of Chicken...,
                       A 5th Portion of Chicken...,
Courlander, Harold   CROWN PUBLISHERS, INC., New York
                       The Heart of the Ngoni, 1982
                       MARLOWE & COMPANY
                       A Treasury of African Folklore, 1996

de Mello, Anthony   IMAGE BOOK, DOUBLEDAY, New York
                       The Song of the Bird, 1982

Erdoes, Richard &   PANTHEON BOOKS, New York
Ortiz, Alfonzo   American Indian Myths and Legends, 1984

Feldman, Christina &   HARPER SAN FRANCISCO
Kornfield, Jack   Stories of the Spirit, Stories of the Heart,
                       1991

Galeano, Eduardo   W.W. NORTON & COMPANY, New York
                       The Book of Embraces, 1989

Hays, Edward   FOREST of PEACE PUBLISHING, INC.,
                          Leavenworth, Kansas
                          The Quest for the flaming Pearl, 1994
                          St. George and the Dragon, 1986
                          The Magic Lantern, 1991
                          The Ethiopian Tattoo Shop, 1983
                          Twelve and a Half Keys, 1981
                          Sundancer, 1982
                          The Christmas Eve Storyteller,
                          The Gospel of Gabriel, 1996

Henderschedt, James   RESOURCE PUBLICATIONS, INC., San
                          Jose, CA
                          The Magic Stone, 1988
                          The Light in the Lantern, 1991

James, Cheewa   HEALTH COMMUNICATIONS, INC,
                          Deerfield Beach
                          Catch the Whisper of the Wind, Stories &
                          Proverbs from Native Americans, 1995

Link, S.J., Mark   TABOR PUBLISHING, Allen, Texas
                          Sunday Homilies, Year A, 1990
                          Sunday Homilies, Year B, Series 1, 1988
                          Sunday Homilies, Year B, Series 2, 1990
                          Sunday Homilies, Year C, Series 1, 1989
                          Sunday Homilies, Year C, Series 2, 1991
                          Daily Homilies, Year I,
                          Daily Homilies, Year II,
                          Daily Homilies, Year I & II, Gospel,

Munsch, Robert   FIREFLY BOOKS, Ltd., Ontario, Canada
                          Love You Forever, 1986

Papineau, Andre   RESOURCE PUBLICATIONS, INC., San
                          Jose, CA
                          Breakthrough, Stories of Conversion, 1970

uoff, Lou

RESOURCE PUBLICATIONS, INC., San Jose, CA
For Give, Stories of Reconciliation, 1991

Sadeh, Pinhas

ANCHOR BOOKS, DOUBLEDAY, New York
Jewish Folktales, 1989

Shea, John

THE CROSSROAD PUBLISHING COMPANY, N.Y.
Gospel Light, Jesus Stories...1998

Smith, S.J., Herbert F.

ALBA HOUSE, New York
Sunday Homilies, Cycle A, 1989
Sunday Homilies, Cycle B, 1990
Sunday Homilies, Cycle C, 1991

White, William R.

AUGSBURG PUBLISHING HOUSE, Minneapolis
Stories for Telling, 1986
Stories for the Journey, 1988
Stories for the Gathering, 1997

OTHER RESOURCES

Dynamic Preaching
Back Issues from
1989 through 2013

SEVEN WORLDS CORPORATION,
310 Simmons Road
Knoxville, Tenn. 37922

Homily Service

Monthly Issues

THE LITURGICAL CONFERENCE, INC.
415 Michigan Avenue, NE
Washington, D.C., 20017-1518

AFRICAN-AMERICAN PREACHING

Philpot, William M.
Smith, J. Alfred

JUDSEN PRESS, Valley Forge
Best Black Sermons, 1972
Outstanding Black Sermons, 1976

Hoard, Walter B.	<u>Outstanding Black Sermons</u> Vol. 2, 1979
Owens, Jr., Milton E.	<u>Outstanding Black Sermons</u>, Vol. 3, 1982
Mitchell, Ella Pearson	<u>Those Preachin' Women</u>, Vol. 1, 1985
	<u>Those Preachin' Women</u>, Vol. 2, 1985
	<u>Women, To Preach or Not To Preach</u>, 1991
Proctor, Samuel D. &	
Watley, William D.	<u>Sermons from the Black Pulpit</u>, 1984
Watley, William D.	<u>From Mess to Miracle</u>, 1989
Cone, James H.	WILLIAM B. EERDMANS PUBLISHING, Grand Rapids, Michigan <u>Speaking the Truth</u>, Ecumenism, Liberation, and Black Theology, 1986
Smith, Sr., J. Alfred	BROADMAN PRESS, Nashville, Tennessee <u>Preach On</u>, 1984, <u>The Overflowing Heart</u>, 1987

CPSIA information can be obtained
at www.ICGtesting.com
Printed in the USA
LVHW021530270620
659107LV00003B/443